First Edition (c) Copyright 2015 Marc W Ford
Second edition (c) Copyright 2017 Marc W Ford
ISBN
978-0-244-92800-1

Thank You

Jem - You know why.

Kieran – You probably know why, but you're now a teenager so I'll give you that knowing look or you'll be embarrassed.

Cover photography by Joe Whitmore @ Joe Whitmore Photography

And to the people who inspire me every day by being genuine and caring when I've had some of my most challenging times.

Index

- Never let a long-term relationship be destroyed over a petty issue.
- Never forget the biggest and most important relationship in your business.

<u>66</u> CHAPTER 4 - Make sure the foundations of your business are strong

- Making your business bigger than one person
- Write a Business Plan - or get someone to write one for you
- Understanding the importance of systems
- Understanding finances - taking control of your business
- Keeping good records always pays off in the long run.

<u>77</u> CHAPTER 5 - Have absolute commitment to your customers

- It's all about respect - if you don't respect your customers don't expect them to come back
- Never lose touch with your customers
- Do you over promise and under deliver?
- The first 30 seconds
- Talk about customer service to your staff - a lot
- Reward good customers
- Keep a notepad in your pocket
- Time - the one commodity that causes the most grief
- Customer expectations are changing - we all need to change with them
- Look at the entire customer service picture - not just little pieces

- Who is your biggest competitor?

CHAPTER 6 - Making your business unbelievable

- Have pride in your workplace (even if you are the only one there)
- Make your workplace inviting and easy for your customers to visit
- Don't scrimp on the little things (out with *Women's Weekly* 1972 or FHM or Countryside Walking Magazine)
- Offer really good coffee and tea (and nice cups)
- Just add laughter (in vast amounts and often)
- Encourage people to bring their personality to work
- Beware of bad smells
- Who is in control of the music?
- Cleanliness is a key component to profitability
- Make one person the keeper of the workplace

CHAPTER 7 - Marketing on a tight budget

- You have to stand out from the crowd
- If your budget is small you need to put in some elbow grease
- Ask people to send you business and they will
- Networking is not a dirty word
- Learn to introduce yourself and your business
- Always be prepared for an opportunity
- Give away products or services to promote your business
- You need to commit time to marketing
- The Internet is here to stay—and it is amazing

- The power of the testimonial
- Do less but do it well

- Do you really know what you are selling?
- Why should someone buy what you are selling?
- To be good at selling you have to be good at listening
- Get someone in to teach your staff how to sell—regularly
- Do you make it easy for people to buy from you?
- How you sold yesterday may not apply to how you sell today or tomorrow
- Become a sales analyser—every time you put your hand in your pocket
- How do you monitor your sales?
- What is the customer's main concern in the sales process?
- Always ask for the sale

- Without this there is no point asking questions
- Question your business partners—ask them to be honest
- Walk around your business—and really look at everything
- Go to successful businesses and find out why they are successful
- Mystery shop your way to success
- Do you charge enough?

- If it doesn't feel right it probably isn't—the business owner's sixth sense
- Talk to your staff—ask them for ideas and their opinions
- Don't be afraid to be a manager—sometimes it's tough
- Write your own operations manual as a way to question what you do

183 CHAPTER 10 - Become the ultimate corporate citizen

- Be involved in the community where you do business
- Look for opportunities outside of the normal
- Stand up and be counted
- Share your knowledge and experience with others
- Encourage your staff to be good corporate citizens
- Some things can't be measured in pounds and pence
- Invest in the future of your industry
- Don't be afraid to tell people you are a good corporate citizen
- Make up a plan to make you the ultimate corporate citizen

194 CHAPTER 11 – Making yourself as impressive as your business

- Appearances are everything
- Have a strong moral code—with no shades of grey
- Be a fair negotiator
- Be more than your business

- Have a life outside of your business
- Be a supporter of other business associates
- Mix with people you can learn from
- Make decisions—procrastination is a killer
- Commit to improving your business skills daily
- Don't be a victim (and keep people who play victim out of your life)

- Believe you are the best and you will become the best
- Enter your business in awards whenever possible
- Get your name in print—there are plenty of opportunities
- Be prepared to get up in front of a crowd—challenge yourself
- Being a green business is good for business
- Be supportive of competitors—even if it is one-sided
- Spend time researching your industry online
- Allow plenty of time to think—and less time to do
- Learn from your mistakes
- Even better, learn from your competitors' mistakes
- Don't become obsessed with your competitors

INTRODUCTION
WHAT TO EXPECT FROM THIS BOOK

When I first wrote this back in 2015, I opened the introduction with this question: 'Are you an entrepreneur?'

At the time I thought it was an interesting question because it was a title that surprisingly very few business owners liked to use. However as time has gone on, the word 'entrepreneur' is in danger of being overused. You are now classed as an entrepreneur if you open a homemade lemonade stand in front of your house during the school holidays or sell other peoples make-up, dietary and skin products on a multi-level basis. It's really called being 'self-employed' or a 'lifestyle business owner'. But anything is possible...so don't let my annoyance with people using the wrong word get in the way.

An entrepreneur, according to the dictionary, is 'a person who sets up a business or businesses, taking on financial risks in hope of profit'. So I'm going take the point of view that because you picked up this book, are looking to succeed and get the edge, then you my friend are indeed an entrepreneur. I took many risks to start my own business and made many mistakes along the way. So as I studied successful businesses and the people that ran them, I figured I should share that knowledge with people who really wanted to reduce the risks they take on a daily basis.

You may be a 'budding entrepreneur' planning to start a business or you may be a seasoned 'veteran entrepreneur' just making sure you haven't missed anything. Both of you and everyone in between are all very welcome!

Being an entrepreneur is exciting, lonely, scary, wonderfully rewarding and incredibly challenging, all in the same breath. To some, it has become a lifestyle choice and there's nothing wrong with that, but if being an entrepreneur is in your blood, it's hard to get it out. As an entrepreneur, you will be more aware than the average person on the street that the better skills, advice and knowledge you get, the greater your chances of business success and the rewards it brings.

Business is getting tough. There are more people starting businesses today than at any other time in history. Since the 2008 crash, nearly half the jobs created in the UK have been classed as self-employed, individual businesses. The micro-business explosion in the last two to three years has become a game changer. There are lots of reasons for this trend with two of the most significant being:

• **Money**: To start a business you need some money behind you. If there are more people with money (or equity in their property) there will be more people starting or buying their own business. In most western countries, at least, the level of affluence is growing substantially and as a result, and so is the number of new businesses starting up. However, this really is a global phenomenon, and business growth is by no means confined to more developed countries. You don't have to start a business with anything physical. You don't have to even open a door, let alone have a door. Heard of the internet anyone?

Did you know the average salary to be 'considered' rich globally is only £15,000?

So before we start...and if you're in an average paid job...well done you! You're already on the road to being rich!

There are many businesses that are busy cutting their cloth, bowing to investor and shareholder pressure, who are trying to SAVE money. There are many reasons for this, but more and more businesses are 'cutting' whole departments and staff numbers so that the balance sheet looks a bit better. The madness of it all is that they then 'outsource' some of the work to freelancers because the departments and the people that they have cut or 'restructured' are still critical to run the business successfully. Take these three areas that are commonly 'cut': Human Resources, Health and Safety and Marketing. All three have evolved at a great pace over the last ten years, and still remain absolutely key to any business success, but are considered 'surplus to requirements' when the finance teams look at the balance sheets.

Without Human Resources, you leave yourself vulnerable to disgruntled employees and tribunals. Without Health and Safety you leave yourself open to days off, poor productivity and an increase in insurance and legal costs. Without Marketing, you are just hoping and praying that adverts hit their target market and a clear message gets to the customers.

Madness. But it leaves opportunities for people who are self-employed.

• Sea change/lifestyle change: For a lot of people the thought of running their own business is far more appealing than going through the grind of working for someone else for the rest of their career. This decision is being fuelled by a general desire to live in a nicer environment, perhaps out of the rat race, and choosing a business that is perceived as being able to deliver a lifestyle to meet these desires.

In my case, I was tired of working for idiot bosses that somehow had got their position by playing politics, rather than actually knowing what they were doing. Some would say that ends up being called leadership, I'd say it's more like making you shake the hand of the right people and jump higher than everyone when someone shouts 'Jump!'

• **Technology:** There is no doubt the world feels a lot smaller.

We are all far more informed and aware of what is happening on a global scale and this is just as relevant for business related issues as it is for world politics.

The increase in technology and communication encourages the entrepreneurial spirit for many people who see what is happening around the world and decide they want to be involved. We read about more business success stories, we watch television shows featuring people making a lot of money from their business and we see new and innovative ideas being turned into reality—on a daily basis.

But what does this mean for you the business owner and entrepreneur?

It means quite simply that anyone in business is going to face a lot of competition and if your business isn't up to speed - look out.

As a business coach and business writer, I spend a lot of time speaking with business owners and entrepreneurs from the UK and around the world, in big business and small business, from just about every industry imaginable. But if you forget the different products being sold, they all share the same pressure of an increasingly competitive market. So this means to succeed you really need to do things better than your competition and that is exactly why I have written this book.

I've written this book because I genuinely want the people who work with me or who read this book to be absolutely brilliant and successful at what they do. My father suffered a failed business in the 1980's recession. It hit our family hard. My mum worked two to three jobs at a time to keep the roof over our head. She missed me and my brother growing up because she was working so hard. It was a horrible place to be.

I bumbled along until the age of 39, when my sister-in-law and mother of three young boys, died suddenly at Christmas. That was the moment I realised I was just wandering around doing things for other people that weren't benefiting me. I realised I hadn't achieved anything of note.

I also realised the stresses and strains that people who work on their own are under. Last year I crashed and burned. I was depressed, worn out and running on empty. More on that later.

So I've come back to this book, adding extra chapters to help take the stress and strain away from you as you move your business forward.

I continue to run events, write books and blogs, present videos and podcasts all aimed at boosting other peoples' businesses, so they don't fail or buckle under the pressure and can be more successful than they perhaps thought.

They've been very successful and I am proud of this fact. They are seen around the world, with their popularity being attributed to their easy delivery of practical tips that can be used by business owners and managers immediately. Well, this book goes one step further- it identifies exactly what the differences are between successful businesses and their owners (those I describe as winning) and those businesses that just never seem to get it right (I call these businesses mediocre).

Success is different for everyone. There are no losers in business...if you think about it, someone, somewhere, always wins. But I do know that if you just implement a few things from this book, you will be in a better place than when you started.

The fact that this book has jumped out at you and found its way into your hands tells me you are already committed to making you and your business 'winning', but sometimes we all need a little help and direction. I'm going to 'nudge' you in the right area, because as one of my clients said, "Marc treats you differently and doesn't treat you like an idiot. You've got this far in one piece, so it's fairly safe to assume, you can only get better". So in this book, I want to put a very significant focus on self-analysing you and your business and actioning the ideas I put forward or that you come up with.

It's all about getting things done. Taking massive action.

If you procrastinate or worse do nothing at all, the competition will catch up and overtake you.

"You may be on the right road...but stand still long enough and you'll get run over."

Sit back, grab a pen and get cracking on what I hope will be some great ideas, thoughts and strategies for you to consider.

What is the difference between success and failure?

This is not an easy question to answer. And it's going to be different for everyone. We can look at a bank account balance but if that was the only indicator we had to measure an entrepreneur's success it would be a sad world indeed. Personally, I believe anyone who is brave enough to step out of their comfort zone and enter the challenging world of self-employment should already be classified as a huge success because there is no doubt that running your own business is tough. If you weren't brave, you would be stacking someone else's shelves or flipping someone else's burgers. There's nothing wrong with that, but you're doing this without a safety net and that is tough.

However, I have noticed that most financially successful entrepreneurs share common personality characteristics and an overriding desire to be great at what they do. I cover these characteristics throughout this book and you may be surprised to notice how many you have. Often this is what drives people to be entrepreneurs in the first place—they are good at what they do and they know it and they would rather make money for themselves than someone else. Or they look at what they are doing and feel they can do better than the restrictions that are placed on them. They find a better way of doing things or make a better end product.

Either way, if I had to pick one defining characteristic that separates success and failure it would have to be passion. Those entrepreneurs who are passionate about their businesses will not accept half-measures - they sincerely want to be the best at what they do.

They are passionate regarding their products and services, their customers and their staff. This passion enables them to embrace change and face the everyday challenges that all business owners face head-on. Yes, they'll encounter setbacks but they don't get caught up in the negatives, preferring instead to move forward, learning from their mistakes and refining the way they do things. They are passionate enough to share their triumphs and tragedies in a philosophical way and they will help other people to succeed wherever they can.

Size really doesn't matter... Honestly, it doesn't!

One of my greatest frustrations is what I call the 'Small Business Syndrome' and I refer to it often. This is where the eternal excuse for not being able to run a business to its full potential is the fact that it is 'only a small business'. From my own experiences, the best run businesses are small businesses and size is certainly no excuse for not providing great service, doing smart marketing, making great products or being innovative and dynamic. Often small business owners are almost apologetic for being a small business.

STOP!

I think it is well and truly time to move on from this mindset and embrace the fact that small businesses are the engine of the business world - there are millions of them and they generally lead the way in all industries.

Being small is no excuse - it is a wonderful opportunity. Imagine being the CEO of a huge multinational corporation - how do you make a change to the way the business operates?

There needs to be countless meetings, often leading to arguments for change, board approval, then the changes need to be handed down to the next level to start the long and winding road to implementation. Once this road is navigated the changes eventually reach the shop floor team that actually sell the product or service. In a small business if you want to make a change—you just do it.

How empowering is that?

My main message here is to be proud of your business, regardless of the size. Building a winning business has nothing to do with size - it is all about you and your attitude.

Do you have the commitment to build a successful business?

As an author, I meet a lot of people who want to write a book. In fact, I am amazed at how many people have this dream. But of all the people who want to write a book very few actually, do it. The real question here is why not?

Coming up with a good idea for a book is pretty easy. I'm sure most of us could sit down with a pen and paper and come up with a few good ideas in a couple of minutes. But what happens once these great ideas are staring back at us from a sheet of paper?

Writing a book takes time, commitment and discipline - just like running a successful business. Running a business is a lot like writing and publishing a book. It's very easy to fall in love with the idea but the reality is that it will take a lot of time, dedication, discipline and hard work just to get it up and running, and then there is no guarantee it will work.

Successful business entrepreneurs have this commitment and dedication and, from my observations, this is a characteristic of their personality type. It is not something they have to decide to do - it just happens.

My advice here is simple: if you're not 100 percent committed to building a very successful business...get a job. Enjoy your weekly pay cheque (there is nothing wrong with that) but don't fall in love with the romantic concept of owning your own business or it will end in tears and heartache.

The best way to use this book.

We all read 'how to' books in our own way. Some people like to start at the beginning and work their way through to the end, point by point. Others prefer to open up at any page and take note of the tip that presents itself, while some others prefer to use the contents page to guide them to the most relevant passages in the book. It really is up to you.

The most important piece of advice I would give you is to make sure you keep an open mind to all of the tips and recommendations made in this book. Think about applying them to your business and visualise the end result of making the change. This is the kind of book that needs to be read and re-read. I believe that often the most pressing issues seem to stand out on the page and it is easy to overlook other recommendations.

But if you put the book down and pick it up again in six months, the issues that were relevant during your first reading have changed and all of a sudden the current issues are the ones standing out on the pages.

Recurring themes

Throughout this book, you will come across a number of themes that are repeated and emphasised. There is a good reason for this: they are very important points. For those people who like to flick from section to section, they will not miss these key points and recurring themes. For those who read a book cover to cover, I don't mean to 'nag'. I'm just reinforcing the key issues for making a mediocre business magnificent and brilliant. Some of these key points include the importance of building strong relationships, the need to be able to promote yourself and your business unashamedly, the need to have good advisers and the need to think like a successful entrepreneur from day one.

Some themes are very tangible, some are more philosophical, but both are equally important. Business success is as much in our heads as it is with the products and services we sell.

Without action, it's all a waste of time

I've written lots of plans for companies all over. They can be detailed plans for large businesses or simpler plans for small business owners. I've coached people into writing many plans, with timelines and responsibilities for actions.

The thickness of the plan is normally proportional to the size of the business and, regardless of this, they look very impressive sitting on the shelf.

But if that is where they stay, they are useless. I love seeing a client's business and asking them to pull out a business plan I helped prepare and it is covered in pen marks, coffee stains, occasionally lipstick (which always has me a little intrigued) and various other signs of human contact. This means the plan is being used - it is being read and reread.

They are questioning recommendations and ideas - reviewing what to do and when to do it. Likewise, the recommendations in this book need to be actioned. They are crying out for it.

I try to make sure I explain how to implement the ideas in a simple, no-nonsense manner. A bit like me!

I've written this book in a slightly different way from others I've gone through in the past. I have included an immediate 'What can you do today?' recommendation at the end of each tip or idea.

This is what you can do today to get your business on track to become winning. Write all over the pages - write on it, anything that comes to mind. Even have a 'mindful doodle' as you may be surprised what 'pops into your head'.

If you action one point every day imagine how much closer your business will be to reaching its fullest potential - an exciting thought.

If one per day is too ambitious, try one per week - the results will be the same, but they will take longer to achieve. So it is up to you.

Remember to delegate if you can (all good entrepreneurs need to be able to delegate) and most important of all, keep this book handy, don't let it gather dust on a shelf.

Share your experiences with others

One of the most impressive characteristics I have noticed among exceptionally successful business entrepreneurs is their very honest and genuine desire to share their knowledge and experiences. I think this is something we should all be prepared to do. Most successful people will be the first to tell you they have made every mistake imaginable (and generally they have made them a number of times over). But the fact that they make these mistakes - which are sometimes quite devastating but they manage to pick themselves up, brush the dust off and then give it another go - is an incredible testimony to their fortitude and conviction. There is nothing more inspirational and motivational than hearing how someone overcame adversity and turned it into success, but for the person telling the story, it is often not that remarkable.

From my own experience, I am constantly surprised by people who want to know my story and background. I feel we all have a very interesting story to get out and inspire others. We have all had a diverse array of experiences that have made us who we are today and these should be exchanged.

Pass on your experiences and knowledge of business and life and you will enjoy the satisfaction of helping other people. Join others, share your experiences and stay in touch, details at the end of the book.

Until then, let's get started and let's get going.

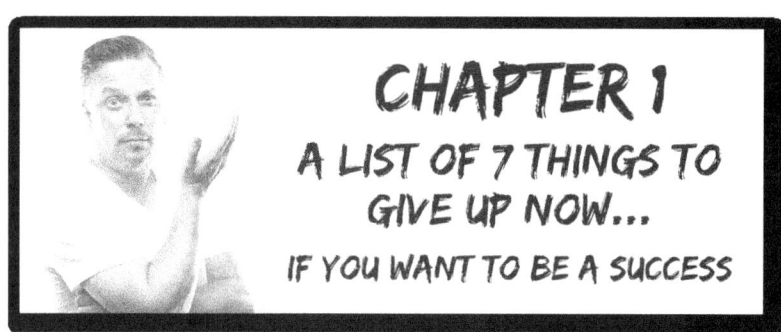

CHAPTER 1
A LIST OF 7 THINGS TO GIVE UP NOW...
IF YOU WANT TO BE A SUCCESS

There are two types of people who read these types of books. And both of them look for something different. The first type of person who wants to read this, are the people who could be looking for an overnight, instant, 100% guaranteed success. Well my friend, look at number one on this list.

The other type of person, which I hope is you, or you are now because you've skipped ahead and looked at number one on the list, is the type of person who is willing to put their back into things and make things work.

So before we get on to the next part of the book which begins to make you look introspectively at your business, I want you to learn to let go a bit. I want to help give you some guidance and ideas, but I don't want you to be resistant to them because you've always had a certain train of thought. It's the 'We've always done it that way...' approach to business. It's this type of approach that leads to things getting old, looking dated and means you get overtaken by your competitors.

One of the misconceptions about business coaches and mentors, in my opinion, is that we 'tell you' what to do. That is not a coach. Coaches share your goals and visions.

They share the fact that you want your business to be as successful as it can be. But they don't share your skills and passion in your chosen area, or any of the emotional baggage that your business generates for you. It doesn't mean we don't care, (we are paid generally on results), but we're more likely to be able to give you a more unemotional perspective of things as they are in reality. And your business is different to the one down the road. Your business is not identical to the big corporate one in a different city. If I were coaching a hairdressing business, could I tell them how to cut someone's hair more productively? God no!

But what I do know is that as a coach I need to open you up to the fresh perspective of looking at what your business is doing now and what it could do in the future with a wide-eyed, no baggage, no fluff approach.

What Can You Do Today?

I want you to take a good look at the following. Now you may find you do one or two of these things. If you ask colleagues or partners they may say all seven!

So what I'd like you to do is be honest with yourself and cut out at least three of the most problematic ones and then see some of the changes that will happen to your business over the next few months.

1. Give up believing that there is a shortcut to success.

If you think you will become successful overnight someday, this is complete bullshit. Miracles like these are impossible and have nothing to do with real life. You have to work hard continuously to get the desired results. Don't believe me?

The amount of people that hold Steve Jobs up as an overnight success is ridiculous. He got fired from his own company. Then they brought him back as it was beginning to fall apart. He asked Apple as a company what they did. The response was, "We make home computers". His reply was something along the lines of let's close the doors then... as they had less than 1% of the home computer market at that time.

Heard of the iPod and the iPhone? Yes, they were a success, but after many years of almost hits, failures, arguments, rows, sackings, and dropping of the ball.

2. Give up your habit of controlling things.

Sometimes things are under your control, sometimes they are not. Don't give undue importance to things which are not in your control. Instead focus on the tasks, objectives and goals you do have full control over. For example, you can control your own attitude, but not others. You can control how you react to a complaint or disagreement, but not control how that person reacts to your points of view.

3. Give up your excuses.

You know you are responsible for everything that happens in your business and your life – good or bad. You know about your strengths and weaknesses and you know the key to success too. You can overcome your weaknesses by limiting your excuses to be successful in any part of your life.

Want that 'six pack' and not the mini-keg or beer barrel you have on the front right now? Eat healthier and do some exercise. It's as simple as that.

Want to earn your first million? Then stop putting off what you know you need to do, or at least go look for some advice on how to get there.

4. Give up the fear of falling down.

Life is all about falling down and getting back up again and so if anyone is afraid of it, forget about tasting success in life. Always remember, fear of failure prevents you from doing anything. You won't be able to make use of any opportunity that comes your way.

In its simplest terms, think back to your childhood, before Health and Safety people in High-Vis jackets ruined our lives. You ran across the playground or tarmac, or field…and fell over! Did you die? No. Did you get back up again, probably with tears in your eyes and some whimpering? Yes. Did you run again? Yes!!

Falling over once did not stop you from running or walking ever again. Imagine the opportunities you'd have missed out on just lay on your back or crawling like a toddler!

It's also as important to realise that you are not invincible. I'm not. No one you know is. As we get older, we buy into doing daft things. We replace the bike by passing our driving test and driving faster than we should. We start drinking, going to nightclubs, drinking to 3 am in the morning, going to bed at 4 am and getting up at 7 am to go to work. We think we can run around without consequences.

So there will be times you need to realise you need to stop, before falling down. The older you get, the more tired, the more stressed, depressed or anxious, the harder it will be to get back up again. So recognise the causes and not the symptoms.

5. Give up saying 'yes' to everything.

In order to accomplish your goal, you will have to learn how to say 'no' and avoid tasks, activities, and demands from your friends, family, and colleagues. At the very least say 'No' to the tasks that gain or get you nothing and get you nowhere nearer your vision and goals.

You have set your priorities and work accordingly. Or else you'll be wasting your most precious commodity…time.

If you are stretched beyond belief, saying 'yes' to everything is a myth. What you are saying 'no' to, will probably not be the best piece of work you'll do. You'll end up hating that way of working. It is not you at your best.

 It will also not be the last bit of work you are given. So don't worry. Always say 'no' to things that don't 'sit' with you comfortably. Whether it is cost, time, quality or even the underlying reason 'why', you need to prioritise what's important and what it means for the bigger picture of your business.

6. Give up your wish to be liked by everyone.

What if nobody likes you? Well, there are at least some that like you I can guarantee that. As I've often been called 'Mr. Marmite', (you either love me or hate me), I used to chase the deluded idea that I wanted to be liked by everyone. I had to stop. It was driving me mad, wasting time, money and energy on people that were never going to like me, be my perfect client or care how I could help them.

There will be a lot of people who don't like you no matter what you did for them and this should not affect you. And there is nothing wrong in this. This is natural, and there's no need to justify yourself to them.

7. Give up your dependency on getting emotional support.

Are you dependent on your friends and colleagues to get emotional support at the time of distress? You don't always need someone. Yes, it's great to get outside help, especially when people rely on themselves too much. They begin to miss the 'woods for the trees'. But it often pays just to close the door, take some time, think with a clear head and just be your own support. Do be introspective and do self-analyse. Just don't do it all day, all the time, otherwise, you begin to lose the will to do things and start to over-analyse instead. It becomes paralysis by analysis.

Now that I've given you a gentle shake, I want you to do your first bit of self-analysis. I want you to fast forward to page 240 and answer as honestly as you can the questions on those pages. Then come back to here.

The biggest thing you'll notice is that when you get to that chapter again, many of your answers will probably different to right now. It shows you that your perspective is beginning to change.

What exactly is a corporate or business image?

It's a term that is often thrown into marketing spiels and books but what does it mean and why is it so important?

Well, the best way to describe the corporate image is that it's the look and feel of your business to potential customers or how your business appears from the outside looking in. For many business people, too much attention is focused looking the other way - from the inside out. So as I've already said, let's take the different perspective of what's going on, by looking outside to in. As a big red alert as to why the customers are not walking in the door, your corporate image could be to blame. But many business owners will find excuses that have nothing to do with them. It's always someone else's fault, isn't it? Wrong.

Your corporate image tells the story of your business. It explains what you do and it positions you against your competitors. There is a lot of psychology associated with corporate imaging - certain words evoke emotional responses; some colours reflect pricing, for example, black and gold are generally associated with cheaper products or services; and the use of particular fonts or style of lettering can make a business look old or modern, professional or amateurish.

Having a good corporate image starts with the name and should permeate through the entire business. Winning businesses live, talk and grow their corporate images. Most winning businesses have very good corporate images, regardless of their size.

If you don't believe me, look at some of the business premises you drive past on a daily basis. Are the ones that look tired, beat up and run down the kind of business you would want to do business with?

No. Unless image renovation is your business of course!

Maybe, just maybe, people are thinking that about your business.
The topics covered in this section include:

- Is your business name telling the right story?
- Do you have a logo and if you do, is it the right one?
- What is your tag line?
- Consistency and the power of branding
- Have you got a good corporate colour?
- Who controls your corporate image?
- There comes a time when you need to review your corporate image
- Corporate imaging in advertising
- A simple task to put things together
- Make sure your team understand your corporate philosophy
- Size doesn't matter - unless you let it
- Have some fun

Is your business name telling the right story?

Choosing the right name for your business is a tough decision. For many new businesses, this is often a major stumbling block. What name should you use?

Before we look at choosing the right name I want to spend a few moments talking about changing your business name.

Over time all businesses evolve. The name you started out with may no longer be applicable to what you do. Many business owners are very hesitant to change their business name if they have had it for a while because they feel they will lose their current customers. I have done some work with various businesses and have recommended they make quite dramatic changes, often including changing the business' name. Not once has this had a negative impact, in fact, quite the opposite: customers like to see a business is changing and evolving, it shows it is progressive and energetic. Large corporations reinvent themselves regularly and their customers almost expect it.

Don't underestimate your customers' ability to cope with change. From my experience, they are better at dealing with it than most business owners. From here you need to decide if your business name really does represent what you truly do. If it does, excellent; if it doesn't, it might be time to make a change.

So what name do you change it to?

There are lots of options. You can choose a clever name, you can choose a simple descriptive name or you can choose a combination of both. Some people like to invent their own word. All are fine options but, remember, if you choose a clever name or a non-descriptive name, you will need to spend more money promoting and branding the business to let prospective customers know exactly what product or services you are selling.

One example I have worked on recently was a florist. This business was well-known and established but it had a similar name to all the other florists in the same region. They mentioned the word florist, flowers or bridal in their names. Looking through the online search engines made it really difficult to pick any one name out because they were all basically the same.

After a creative session, we came up with the name 'Buds'. It's a short, simple and modern name that reflected the owner's style and beliefs perfectly. They now had a name that was easy to remember, distinctive and fresh. Their business has never looked back.

The decision you need to make is: do you want to be more interesting or more functional?

I am certainly not advocating either, just explaining the choices. Ideally, coming up with something in the middle, a creative but explanatory style of name, is the easiest to build a brand around and to let customers know what you do.

Whatever your business name is or whatever name it is going to become, getting customers to use the business quickly is the difference between losing money over a short time or over a long time.

What can you do today?

Review your business name.

Does it truly represent what you do?
Is it well known?
Is it right for the direction you are planning to take your business?

If it is great, this is still a good exercise to do. If it isn't now is the time to do something about it. Start planning your new business name and how you will go about changing it. Put some thought into it, ask customers, staff, friends and family, but make your own decision. Remember resistance to change will always be there but this resistance needs to be overcome for the long-term growth and success of your business. Winning businesses have good logos and strong corporate images because they know how important they are. Think about the logos of companies you deal with. Look through newspapers or magazines and check out the logos of the larger organisations. There is nothing stopping any sized business from having a strong, corporate image. Those that do will reap the rewards.

When deciding on which graphic designer to use, contact a few. Most have websites these days where you can check out their past logo designs. Try to find one whose style you like and ideally show them what type of logos you like. Negotiate a price up front so you know how much it will cost. Remember also that you will need to incorporate the new logo on your stationery and promotional material, so you may wish to plan the introduction of a new logo when your current stocks are low.

If you are changing your existing logo, make a big deal of it. Let your customers and suppliers know what's happening. Take ownership of it and be proud of your new corporate image.

Do you have a logo and if you do, is it the right one?

A logo is simply a graphical image used to promote your business. For some businesses it is a symbol of some sort, for others, it is just the name in a stylised font and for some, it is a combination of both. Logos are excellent tools for carrying a unique theme through your business and this is the very essence of a good corporate image.

Logos need to be distinctive and unique to your business. In my business, I use a crisp set of lettering with light blue and orange. The blue I associated with a crisp, fresh feel; the orange with the fire in my belly for success and I think the end results are very memorable - the message is: if you use my business we will give you some fresh ideas to use in your business. It's a simple message but one that appears to be working extremely well. All of our promotional material, stationery, signage and websites use the logo to carry through our corporate image.

One of my major gripes with many modern, smaller businesses is the lack of quality logos or, worse, logos designed at home by someone who really has no idea what they are doing. If you are starting a new business, allocate a budget to developing a good logo. If you are in business and you haven't got a logo or you have a pretty ordinary logo, today may be the day to commission a graphic designer to come up with one that is memorable and distinctive.

What can you do today?

If you haven't got a logo, get one!
If you have one and it is tired, amateurish or no longer current get cracking on developing a new one.

What is your tagline?

A tagline is basically a few simple words that make a statement about your business. All businesses can use a tagline and the best advice I can give about choosing one is that it should answer the customer's question, 'Why should I use your business?' And keep it short and sharp.

Trends come and go, taglines go in and out of fashion like colours, but I think they have considerable merit. Taglines can be altered as your business changes or as the market in which you do business changes. Like choosing a name for your business, trying to define a simple tagline is not an easy task but the two should go hand in hand.

I recommend buying a book called 'Words that sell' by Richard Bayan if you are looking for inspiration to help you with determining a tagline. This excellent publication is recommended extensively by advertising agencies, marketing companies and copywriters looking for words on a daily basis.

What can you do today?

If you have a tagline, review and assess if it still works.
If you haven't got one, get one!
Go out right now and purchase a copy of 'Words That Sell' and get those creative juices flowing.
Run a competition among your staff or customers for ideas and/or ask your family, friends or business network for advice.

Consistency and the power of branding

Branding is one of those words we hear a lot. 'Developing a brand', 'building a brand', 'brand value' and so on... Most people think branding is applicable only to large businesses but it isn't. It is equally important for small businesses and business people.

Any business can build a brand. Put simply this means when a consumer sees your company name (and logo) they have a positive perception of the business. This is one of the most appealing aspects of buying a franchise - you are purchasing an accepted brand name that consumers will hopefully already know and have a positive opinion about. Clearly, it takes time to build a brand and to develop brand awareness but we all need to do it.
The real key to branding is consistency: sending a consistent message through your advertising, corporate image and look of your business. This affects the appearance of your business and all areas where your business interacts with consumers.

Consistency is controlled by systems - having the right mechanisms in place to ensure all aspects of your business are consistent is the starting point. Later in this chapter, I discuss how to control your brand and assign an individual to this task, but the term consistency in all aspects of the business needs to be driven from the top.

Now I know I have also discussed that change is a good thing in corporate imaging but I would like to clarify this. Having a current, relevant and impressive corporate image is essential to making a winning business. When the change is made, you need to build your corporate image and your brand with consistency in all that you do.

What can you do today?

Have a look at your business and all that is involved with it. In what areas could you become more consistent in your branding?
Make a list and start working through them one by one.

Have you got a good corporate colour?

A big part of a strong corporate image is having a strong corporate colour. This means there is generally one dominant colour used in all aspects of your corporate image. This dominant colour is used consistently in everything you do and it forms the basis of the business' promotional material.

Different colours evoke different emotions and it is important to choose an appropriate colour for your business.

Darker colours tend to give a stronger, more established feel, hence a lot of law firms and accountants use dark blues, browns and even black as their corporate colour. Lighter colours tend to reflect a more modern look and feel and they are often favoured by businesses in the creative fields. This is an area where you need to take the advice of a good graphic designer. Decide what image you want to portray and then get them to turn it into a colour.

Colours, like most aspects of corporate branding, can go in and out of fashion so your corporate colours will need to be changed periodically. Just like a logo, they have a finite lifespan. Make sure the colour you choose can be used consistently in all printing and advertising as some colours are harder and more expensive to reproduce. Orange is one prime example of this; you can end up with a lot of variations which may erode the overall strong and consistent image you are trying to portray.

Here are some examples of 'colour psychology':

Red:
Emoting strength, passion and excitement

Use in marketing terms:
Used extensively in food terms to trigger appetite
Conveys a strong energy
Attracts attention and adds visibility

Companies that use it:
Virgin, Coca-Cola

Yellow:
Emoting intellect, joy and energy

Use in marketing terms:
Conveys positivity, high energy and optimism
Stimulates creativity and attracts customer attention
Indicates fun and a cheerful brand

Companies that use it:
McDonalds, Ferrari

Blue-
Emoting loyalty, trust and intelligence

Use in marketing terms:
Considered the most popular brand colour
Suggest high loyalty and precision
Closely associated to intelligence and trust

Companies that use it:
Ford,Dell

Green-
Emoting freshness, growth and safety

Use in marketing terms:
Is considered the easiest for human vision
Used to project an easy, relaxed image and environment
Extensive use for environmental projects

Companies:
Starbucks, Whole Foods

What can you do today?

If you have a corporate colour, evaluate if it is still appropriate and correct for what you do.

If you don't have a specific corporate colour, choose one, ideally with the help of a professional such as a graphic designer. Their role is to be a central point of reference to approve promotional material and advertising for the individual operators within the chain, ensuring all material is consistent with the determined corporate image. This creates a very professional and consistent corporate image and makes sure consumers are being sent the right message.

On a smaller scale, keeping control of your corporate image is equally as important. Over time it can easily start to erode as different fonts are introduced, the colours of the logo start to vary and the layout of promotional material differs each time it is produced. Ideally, one person should be used to control all aspects of your corporate image.

Their job is to:

• make sure the logo appears in the right format every time
• make sure the colours used are correct and consistent

- ensure the same font is used in promotional material
- ensure the format of details, such as telephone numbers and addresses, is consistent
- sign off on all proofs for advertising and promotional material
- control the use of words to make sure of consistency of copy
- keep copies of all promotional material and advertisements to form a historical library
- control the use of images—for example, always send copies to avoid losing originals.

Who controls your corporate image?

Believe it or not, there are companies that specialise in controlling corporate image. These are generally used by large organisations, such as hotel chains, big banks and other brands.

Being a small to medium or a start-up business, this isn't going to happen. So you must decide what the image is, what it needs to convey and who is going help you do it. Just as importantly who is going to keep it looking the same across all the channels that you use? From social media to websites; from brochures to letterheads; from banners to posters; it all needs to be consistent.

What can you do today?

Decide how you will control your corporate image and most importantly who will control your corporate image.

There comes a time when you need to review your corporate image

Corporate images need to change. Over time they become dated, they lose their impact and to be honest they can often start to look amateurish. There is no set period of time between corporate image changes, it is more a matter of realising when the existing image has had its day and no longer truly represents the business. A lot of businesses struggle with making changes to the corporate image. There is an underlying concern that if they change their corporate image they may lose customers resistance to change or a genuine belief that their customers could go somewhere else simply because the business introduces a new logo or even a new name.

The reality is that customers like to see businesses changing their corporate image - it shows the business is innovative and keeping up with the times. It shows that the business owners are proud of their business and they are prepared to reinvest in it. I've not seen a new corporate image that hasn't been a very positive step in the history of a business. A new image reinvigorates everyone - the business owners, the staff and even the customers.
It is in its own right a sign of business success.

Another common mistake I see is the business owner who has developed their own logo and corporate image on their home PC and they think it is sensational. Sure, sometimes people can develop great logos at home, but more often than not the end result is a long way from the desired professional result and the business' corporate image is terrible.

Spend some money and get a professional logo developed, and get the right advice on the use of colours and the design of promotional material. Saving a few pounds on the design of a strong corporate image is not a smart move and in most cases, it ends up being a false economy as the business struggles to attract customers from the start.

Corporate imaging in advertising

Is your corporate image accurately recreated in your advertising?

For many businesses, advertising is done on an ad hoc basis, with no real direction. The end result can be that the advertising does not carry the corporate image through. Look at your advertising and see if it carries your corporate image through in a consistent manner.

If it does great, but could it be improved?
If it doesn't what can you do to make it happen?
Should your logo be more prominent?
Should the style of the font being used be more consistent or unique?

There are lots of ways to build a corporate image into your advertising and a good graphic designer is essential to guide you through the process.
This means it is harder for potential customers to form an association between your advertising and your business.

Have a good long hard look at your existing corporate image, specifically your logo, your sign writing and your promotional material. Compare it to your competitors and be brutally honest.

Ask your business associates, staff and customers if they think it needs to be updated and ask them for an honest and candid opinion. It might be fine, but it might be time to set the wheels in motion to start developing your new corporate image. If you do need some changes made, contact your local graphic designers and make appointments for them to come in and show you what they can do.

Just like all aspects of corporate imaging, your advertising should be consistent and carry the 'look and feel' of your business. Over time this helps to build the effectiveness of your advertising - people see your advertisements and recognise straight away that they relate to your business. Look at the advertising done by large corporations. You will clearly see that their advertising follows a distinct format designed to be easily recognisable as belonging to them. It is important to overcome the urge to change your advertisements regularly simply for the sake of it.

Consumers are bombarded with thousands of advertising messages every day and for advertising to really work it needs time to sink in. If you send a constantly changing message or a confusing message, where the consumer has to try and figure out who the advertisement belongs to, they will simply switch off.

Spend a few minutes looking through your local newspaper and see which advertisements you can identify with a specific company within the first second of looking at it. This is the image we all need to portray.

Assess what makes the advertisement so easily recognisable. The colours used, the size of the logo, the type of font used, the pictures used or even the location of the advertisement itself?

If you are not sure how to carry your corporate image through your advertising enlist the services of a good graphic designer. Explain to them exactly what it is you are trying to achieve and they will do the rest.

A simple task to put things together.

Now what you've already been given maybe making your head spin or whizz. I understand that. But you have no idea how important all this stuff is. People can stumble upon many things, but a good image and how it's portrayed is not one of them. It takes time and a thought process. You want people to buy from you. You want people to come to you. Some marketing feels so unbelievably desirable that you just can't wait to pull out your credit card and make a purchase.

Smart marketers know and understand how to find that unique style that connects their target market and drives them to action. The question is; how do you find a style that suits your personality, business and your customers?

This is a simple task to get you thinking.

Answer the following questions on your business and this will not only assist you in finding your unique style, it will also help you in establishing a 'style guide' for your business overall. This means that every time you send out a marketing campaign, take a telephone call, speak from the stage, market online you refer back to the core styles that your business possess.
This kind of consistency across the board is what makes a winning business profitable.

Answer these questions:

1. If my business were a person, what kind of person would it be?
2. What kind of personality would it possess?
3. How would it engage with others?

4. What would its top 3 brand values be? (i.e. what does it stand for?)
5. What would its top 3 personality traits be? (i.e. fun, quirky, humorous etc.)

Putting a personality to your business means that your communication style and the way you talk to your potential clients and customers, becomes unique to that of others and more appealing.

Take Virgin as an example. Virgin is fun, adventurous and costs saving.

Businesses that suffer from lack of cash flow, typically do so because their message isn't unique or memorable.
It is also worth mentioning here that slogans and brand values aren't just for big business either.
When applied to even the smallest of businesses, the way their prospective market perceives them suddenly shifts.
It's this shift in perception that can be in many instances what a business needs for it to turn around.

Many in their rush to make money will try Facebook. Google AdWords, newspaper adverts and other advertising options, thereby wasting thousands, but without this core aspect successfully put in place, it doesn't matter how much you market and spend, it won't get you the optimal result you desire unless it's clear and memorable.

So 'WHAT' does your business stand for?
Define it to 3 top brand values only, such as;
'Entrepreneurial, Engaging, Effective'

Now it's your turn...
• Brand Value #1:
• Brand Value #2:

- Brand Value #3:

Write these in big letters and stick them to your desk. Be sure to include emotions within the top 3 brand values. Because people buy feelings by purchasing a particular product or service that makes them feel a certain way, i.e. L'Oreal, "Because you're worth it!"

Whenever you send out marketing material, your material must reflect these 3 core values and, even more importantly, these values must be communicated via the use of a slogan used to represent your business as a whole.

What can I do today?

Do the above and work towards helping you create a strong consistent message across the board. With consistency comes trust which equals higher conversion rates and increased sales in your business. Not to mention, potential clients and customers remembering precisely who you are and what you stand for and why you're different. Once you have your list, turn it into a reality and introduce these new ideas into your business.

Make sure your team understand your corporate philosophy.

All too often the head of an organisation knows where it is going but the tail is never told - it just has to follow blindly and hope for the best.
What is your philosophy?

Corporate philosophy - some people may call this your mission statement but I personally think it's more. Where do you see your business being in one year, five years, ten years and even fifty years? Write this down.

This may be a simple, one-page document which outlines what your business will look like in the future, including what you will sell, where the business will be located, how many staff you will have, what your role in this organisation will be over this timeframe.

Once you know what your vision is, take the time to explain it to the people you work with. Share the vision so they know where you are going. They may not be as passionate about it as you but that isn't their job. Even if you don't have any staff, it is good for you to know where you are going to be.

I used to work for a company that had a hundred-year vision in place. This was a huge corporation, but they were very clear on where they were going. They had factored in good times, bad times, wars, political changes, world epidemics, and the lot. Quite an amazing document to read and it certainly gave me a sense of belonging to an organisation that knew where it was going. Even if the road ahead had no guaranteed direction, their final destination was very clear.

What can you do today?

Write your own corporate or business vision - where do you want to be in the future? It could cost almost one million pounds for the design alone; for a small business, it can be as little as a few pounds on certain websites.
Winning entrepreneurs know the value of looking the part and they realise that investing in a good corporate image is just one of the steps involved in building a successful business.

Size doesn't matter—unless you let it

This is one of those points that I emphasise a lot in all of my coaching. Don't let the size of your business prevent you from doing it right. You don't need to be a big corporation to have a good corporate image. I have played a significant role in developing strong corporate images for countless small businesses and, yes, they have invested a significant amount in the image but they have all built much stronger businesses as a result of this investment. In fact, I would go one step further and say that it is much easier for a smaller business to develop a good corporate image than it is for a larger organisation.

Imagine the decision-making process: a small business may have only a couple of people to make the final decision, so the process is short; a big corporation can have an endless decision-making process that will make the task almost impossible and often it is, hence any change takes a long time to develop.

Costs are proportional. Developing a new logo for a large multi-national corporation can be a huge pain in the backside. It goes through meetings, committees, politics and presentations galore. It takes time and money. If you're a small business, you can approach local designers, or websites that can have much quicker turnaround times and doesn't need the approval of hundreds of people, just the ones that matter.

It's not that serious - have some fun!

I am a very firm believer that business should be fun. Sure there are plenty of times when this is easier said than done, but some businesses just seem to lack any joy at all. I can't imagine working in an environment like that for hours on end, day after day, month after month. I think some people confuse professionalism with being serious. It is not unprofessional to have a workplace where people like to laugh and enjoy themselves. As a customer, it is much more enjoyable to walk into a light, friendly, energetic environment than a serious, gloomy and uncomfortable environment.

Fun takes many different shapes but I believe very strongly that it should be welcomed into all businesses and I do believe it is a key component of many of the leading winning businesses I have observed. For me, it is a real joy to see modern entrepreneurs, such as Richard Branson, who are such key advocates of promoting fun for staff and customers. Sure we all have stressful times, we all have to balance money, deal with unhappy customers, manage staff problems and a host of other everyday issues, but it really isn't that serious. Have some fun at work, encourage other people to do likewise and you and your business will enjoy the benefits for many years to come.

What can you do today?

There is a lot here to think about. Go into it with a sense of humour. The winning businesses don't take themselves too seriously. Sir Richard Branson dresses up in wedding dresses to promote his business. If you ask 'Siri' certain questions it comes up with funny answers and that's from a company that is an international giant.

Make up a list of five things you could do to introduce more fun into your workplace and your business. If you struggle to find five things, ask your staff or ask your customers. There is nothing wrong with asking other people for ideas.

CHAPTER 3

BUILDING STRONG RELATIONSHIPS...

KNOW, LIKE, TRUST AND DO BUSINESS

To succeed in business you are going to need to build strong relationships with a lot of different people. These relationships will help your business grow, they may help you through difficult times and they will also bring a lot of enjoyment to your business life. Like any relationship, they need to be built over time and with mutual trust. This chapter deals with building relationships to help you succeed in your entrepreneurial life.

The topics covered include:

- Who do you want to have a strong relationship with?
- Always check references of potential suppliers
- Take the time to get to know the people you want to build a relationship with
- Loose lips sink ships and sometimes businesses, but silence is golden
- Never let a long-term relationship be destroyed over a petty issue.
- Never forget the biggest and most important relationship in your business.

Who do you want to have a strong relationship with?

A very distinct observation and experience I've made of successful businesses are that the owners are generally very good at building relationships with everyone they deal with. They seem to have the PR button on their personality permanently switched on. It's almost sickening!

They seem to get on with their staff, their customers, their suppliers, their landlords, their bank and their professional advisers, such as lawyers and accountants. These people clearly understand that to create a successful business it takes more than one individual - it takes a team or a network with many components, each equally important. Often entrepreneurs can overlook some relationships or not really give them the attention they need. One example that comes to my mind in this respect is banking. Somewhere I worked in my chequered career.

Like most people, I assumed, before I worked there that the days of having a relationship with your bank manager were long gone. Before I joined the company, I had been with one of the big banks for many years and never really considered changing because I thought all banks were the same. This caused me a lot of problems: I struggled to get an overdraft, I didn't have a personal contact who could advise me on various financial matters and I really looked at banking as an irritation rather than a relationship building opportunity.

That all changed when I went to work for one. I was trained by a few account managers but the one I learnt the most from was a woman called Anita. A bubbly, vivacious woman, married to a police officer I seem to recall.
She had been in this inner town branch of the business for a few years.

She knew her customers. She knew about their lives and she knew about their trials and tribulations.

She had built a relationship of trust with all of them. We even had people just popping into the branch to come and say 'hello'. When was the last time you did that to your bank manager?

During this process, I got to learn a lot about this impressive way to do business and before long I was watching her techniques and observing her personal skills. All of a sudden I became a bank manager who not only knew your name but also took an active role in your business so I could potentially do business with you later.

Anita was one of my unofficial mentors - an honest and open woman who has helped my career to grow - and I will be grateful to her forever. It got me a promotion, several bonuses and I won several incentives.

The point I am trying to make here is that we shouldn't necessarily believe everything we read, in this case, about banks. They are certainly not all the same and the opportunity does exist to forge a relationship if you can find the right person. The same applies to virtually everyone you deal with, but you have to be open-minded to let a relationship form - it takes trust and effort.

Every time a customer comes into your business they are putting their trust and faith in you; that you will meet their expectations. If you do they will keep coming back. If you work with your suppliers to develop a mutually beneficial relationship, they will reciprocate.

Just as it is important to try and build relationships there are bound to be some people who you just can't deal with or meet their expectations. In this case, there will be no relationship and that is okay. Let it go and move on; hopefully, these situations will be minimal.

Make the effort and put some energy and thought into the cogs that make your business go round and determine the benefits to you and to them of your relationship being stronger.

What can you do today?

Make a list of the people who form the network that is your business. Besides these people or companies names rate your current relationship. Look at the ones that need improving and make a plan that outlines how you will make these relationships stronger.

Always check references of potential suppliers

A good supplier of goods or services is an important part of the overall running of a successful business. Having a strong relationship with them is important and a good start will help the relationship grow in a positive manner.

When setting up accounts with suppliers it is very likely they will want to do a check on you or your business to make sure you are able to pay their bills.

You will probably have to supply a lot of your personal details, trade references verifying your business is good at paying its bills and a personal guarantee from the business owners or directors, which means if the business goes bankrupt they will be personally liable for any outstanding monies owed.

I think it is equally important you know your suppliers are reputable and most importantly that they will deliver what they say they will. Clearly, you don't have the same financial risk as the supplier does when dealing with your business but it is important for you to do some homework and establish that this will be a good relationship for your business and ultimately your customers.

Based on this I recommend that when setting up accounts you ask the supplier to give you the names of some of their customers who can verify they will deliver what they promise when they promise it.

Social proof, checking Facebook pages and review pages is also a great idea. But be warned...there is not a company on the face of the earth that won't have a negative review about them. Remember a key thing about reviews and review sites. Not many people go onto them to place 'O.K.' reviews. Like many things there are extremes. You just need to take a look at something like 'Trip Advisor'. The negative reviews and the super-duper reviews certainly outweigh the 'it's alright' reviews. There is very little middle ground.

So remember as hard as anyone tries, we can't please all the people all the time. If there is a negative review or comment, check how they've responded to it.
Many companies will not do this and that often makes me wonder why not?

What are they hiding? If they are proud of their business they would want to put it right as quickly as possible and redress the negative image the comments or review has given them.

Businesses want all of your details but they won't give you any of theirs. Not a fair transaction if you ask me.

If your suppliers let you down, you will probably end up letting your customers down. Your customers won't blame the supplier, they will blame you, and this can affect the long-term success of your business.

Take the time to get to know the people you want to build a relationship with.

Building strong relationships takes time. Once you identify the people or the businesses that you want to build relationships with you also need to allocate time to get to know them. Now I am not suggesting you move in with them, just that in the course of your daily business you find out a little more about them.

I am going to be honest with you. Not every person you come across will want to help you with your business. They will take what they can and move on. They will want you to succeed at their pace or on their terms.

It becomes a hard life lesson and sometimes a bitter pill to swallow, so to make things seem a little clearer on what I mean I'm going use a story that I read in a book called 'Act Like A Success, Think Like A Success' by American comedian Steve Harvey.

The analogy is called "Man on a Rope"

'For those of us trying to become successful, our journey can be compared to the task of putting a wagon up a steep hill.

Those willing to make the climb are typically business leaders, business owners, heads of families, foundation heads or leaders of children.

This wagon is like a wooden wagon that you may have seen in westerns.

Our responsibility is to pull that wagon up the hill. This wagon doesn't have any rubber wheels on it. It doesn't have a motor. It doesn't have metal spokes. It's just an old wagon that you are pulling up a very steep Hill.

It has no horse in front of it. It doesn't even have a donkey in front of it. It just has a very thick single rope. Think of one that you could find in a PE lesson…except it's twice the size. The rope is so thick it will cut your hands…yes you are pulling this wagon.

Your trousers are torn to shreds and filthy. This is a climb you are doing barefoot and the ground underfoot is likely to give way at any time. You are sweating like a pig in an abattoir. The rope is on your shoulder and its rubbing and cutting deep.

What makes your journey more challenging is the weight and expectation of the people that are riding the wagon. You are carrying them with you on your journey.

But here's the thing - the people on this wagon are the ones that only YOU allow to ride with you.

If you are smart you will only choose people that will help you move this wagon up the hill. You don't want a wagon full of dead weight. No one else can pull this wagon but you. You are the one that wants to become successful. Remember you are the one with a vision. So the question is…who do you want on your wagon?

People can help you climb, but they can't pull the rope for you. What you are looking for are people that are happy to push with one leg. They are not strong enough to push you entirely…they have their own wagons to pull on a different hill.

You have some people that can feed you. Mop your brow. They will even be willing to kick rocks out of the way for you.

At night, the wagon is still attached to you. You can't let go. If you take a rest, you can't lean back, because the people are still on the wagon. It's still heavy even when you are sleeping.

Your closest people are allowed to inspire you, encourage you and give you the strength to carry on…but they cannot pull the wagon. They cannot pull for you…the rope and the wagon are yours alone.

Your people in your wagon should play various roles to contribute towards the successful journey, otherwise, why have them on board?

You need someone to count your money. You need someone to provide you with some sort of counsel. The problem is that when some see you not looking they will stop helping. Some get so good, they lie in the middle of the wagon and….well…just lie there and just ride.'

So the questions are…

WHO are you allowing on your wagon?

WHAT are they doing to help you nearer your vision and your goals?

So do these people display the behaviours that you want to be associated with?

Are they still useful or have they stopped being helpful?

If I had this wagon the very least I'd want someone to do is to put some lotion on the rope, making it softer and less harsh. Someone who can fix a broken wheel. Repair the wagon. Make a cover for it when it rains.

It's not often things have a real effect on me, but this story is so simple and yet absolutely on the money for those who want to succeed and believe in their vision and what relationships should be like in business terms.

So you could ask, what is the best way to talk to people, especially new business associates?

I was a bit lame at it myself if I'm honest. Let's be fair everyone's favourite subject is themselves and I couldn't stop talking about myself. So you can imagine that I didn't 'control' networking or business conversations very well. That was until I tripped over a book by American businesswoman and millionaire Dani Johnson.

She came up with a really simple, (most of the best ideas are, aren't they?), formula of how to talk and control conversations in a networking environment.

By really getting to know the person you're talking to and what makes them tick, they feel you are interested in them as people and not as another statistic in your sales book. This way they are going to trust you and want to hear what you have to say. They are going to be open to hearing your message.

Remember, you are focusing on relationships and business development.

You can do this by asking questions using something called 'FORM'.

"F" stands for family.
"O" stands for occupation.
"R" stands for recreation.
"M" stands for message.

Asking people about their family, occupation, and recreation is a way to find out what people are interested in and to show interest in them. Remember that people's favourite subject is themselves, so get people talking about those three simple things.

#1: Family. Ask them where they're from. Are they married or single? How long have they been married? Do they have any kids? Ask them to tell you about them. What are their ages? What do they like to do? How long have they lived in the area? Do they like where they live? Things like that.

#2: Occupation. Ask them what they do for a living. How long have they been doing it? What do they like about it and what don't they like? How did they get started in that profession? Do they see themselves in that profession forever? What are the good things about it? What are things that are terrible about it? If they could change anything in their profession, what would it be?

#3: Recreation. What do they like to do for fun? How often do they get to do it? With whom do they like to do it? How did they get interested in that recreational activity that they like to do, whether it's golfing or football or travelling or knitting or crocheting or painting or singing or dancing or writing?

The last step in FORM is **#4 Message.** You share your message after you find out all about them, and then you introduce them to your presentation. The goal is to put the focus on the other person and take the focus away from you.

(F.O.R.M. is taken from Dani Johnson's Book 'First Steps to Wealth'. Read more about Dani's story at www.danijohnson.com)

What can you do today?

Make it a policy in your business that any new suppliers of goods or services must supply references you can check to make sure they will deliver according to their promises. If they won't do this then find another supplier - there are plenty out there.

People who are good at building relationships are often good at building businesses.

They are genuinely interested in the people they deal with. They take the time to get to know them and by showing an interest the relationship grows naturally anyway.
Think about the people who come into your business on a daily basis and perhaps have done so for years.
What do you know about them?

For example, the courier who has been picking up and dropping off deliveries for the past twelve months, do you even know their name, where they live, what they did before they became a courier, what they like to do on weekends or what their plans are for the future?
Today's courier could be tomorrow's customer.

Spend a little time to get to know the people you do business with and do it sincerely. They will respond in a positive manner and your interactions will be more enjoyable for both parties. They are more likely to go the extra mile if you need them to. They are also more likely to tell other people about your business. All of a sudden you will have another free sales rep promoting your business.

Loose lips sink ships and sometimes businesses.

While I am advocating the importance of building relationships there need to be some very clear boundaries established. In most business relationships there should be limits on what information you pass on or talk about as there is always the possibility the person you are talking to is going to walk out of your business and into your competitors' and tell them everything. I don't want to sound paranoid, but I have personally experienced this.

I once spoke to someone about a project I was tendering for. I discussed prices and the outline of my tender only to find out that a last-minute submission by a competitor got the job because they were cheaper. I did a little research and found out that the brother of the person I confided in worked at the competitors' business. A coincidence?

Not likely, even though that can be the nature of doing business. I learned a valuable lesson from this and moved on, but since then I have been much more cautious about what I tell people.

Further to this a lot of people confide in me about their business. What would happen to my reputation if I didn't honour their trust and started giving away their trade secrets? I've dealt with lots of businesses and all of them run them in different ways. There are some genuinely brilliant ideas being worked on as we speak in various industries, but is it right for me to tell others about them if

they are in the same industry? No. Would it be right for me to claim them as my own and make myself out to be a complete business genius? No.
This is a quick way to develop an unethical reputation.
So in short, build relationships but keep your cards a little closer to your chest.

No matter how close the relationship appears to be, there are some things that should not be shared as your integrity is on the line.

What can you do today?

Think about how much information you or your staff, partners or colleagues pass on. Is it too much?

Does your team have clearly defined boundaries on what information they can share and what information is considered confidential and not to be given out for any reason?

If not, today is the day to clarify this point.
Life is too short to get stressed and bent out of shape every time something goes wrong with a supplier or work associate. Work with the people you have good relationships with and your business will enjoy the benefits.

Never let a long-term relationship be destroyed over a petty issue. All too often a very strong relationship can be ruined over a very small issue.

Things can go wrong in business, we all know that, but don't let a perfectly good relationship suffer or end because of an issue that in the scheme of things is quite petty.

If you have a great relationship with a supplier and they mess up on one shipment, they deserve another chance. After all, everyone makes mistakes and while they are embarrassing they are generally not the end of the world.

On a similar note, don't take any crap. There are some great people in business. But just like the school playground, there are some complete idiots and bullies. I've been there and done that. There were some downright nasty people that tried to destroy my fledgling business some time back.

They thought it fair to make comments to other professionals, suppliers and sponsors about my private life. It affected my family. Comments were made to them in the street, on social media and even worse my son's school. That is NOT on.

You can stand the odd bad review and the odd comment or even phone call, but please don't let it affect you or your family or your employees.
There is a professional out there that can deal with unprofessional people like that...they're called solicitors.

What can you do today?

Think about the relationships you have in your business. Would they survive a petty dispute?
Have you lost a good relationship because of a small issue that got out of hand?
Have you sat back, been bullied or had your reputation damaged by someone that was completely unprofessional?

Think about how you would handle the same situation in the future and keep this thought in the back of your mind for the next time a situation threatens a relationship.

(Another great read on relationships in business is the book called 'Snakes in Suits: When Psychopaths Go to Work', Paul Babiak and Robert D. Hare)

Never forget the biggest and most important relationship in your business.

This relationship is so very important and very much overlooked by everyone, until things go wrong.

This relationship is more important than the one with friends and family. It's massively important not to rely on those people but to have people around to let off steam with. If things go wrong, the love and support from your friends and family are very, very healthy and humbling. They will be there to get you 'out of your funk' and help you see things more clearly. And if you're a massive success, they will be there to help you celebrate. There is a never a truer word spoken when people say "It's lonely at the top...", so why become another statistic? Success isn't all about money. It's just as much about the quality of the life you have outside of the business.

But apart from friends and family, I am yet to mention the most important relationship in your business. It's with yourself. The most important asset in your business. Without you...there is no business.

We are constantly pushed to remember this, remember that. Be here, be there. Do this, do that. And all of it for other people, who generally don't give a crap about you or your business.

We spend hundreds, thousands, tens of thousands, even hundreds of thousands on things that make our businesses run properly. We take time and effort to get them to work as efficiently as they can do, but perhaps we are all guilty of not taking the time and effort to manage the most important part of the business; ourselves.

What can you do today?

Schedule some time for you. Get a relationship with your mind and your body.
Go to the gym. Go for a walk.
Take the morning off. Take a day off.
Recharge your batteries.
Respecting yourself as much as you respect any other part of your business is vital to your business success.

Listen to your mind and body. If it doesn't feel right, take advice. Not respecting yourself is worse than abusing any relationships you may have. So schedule some time to be with you...just you. Your business will thank you for it.

CHAPTER 4

MAKE SURE THE FOUNDATIONS ARE STRONG

SO YOU CAN BUILD IT AS BIG AS YOU LIKE

Most businesses evolve over time. At the start, there isn't a lot of structure or planning and the needs of the business influence any changes. It almost becomes a Warner Brothers cartoon, where the character puts one finger in the dam, then another hole pops up, and they fill that with a finger, then another opens up and they fill that with a toe and then another opens and so on...well that's how it feels.

As it grows the operation and how it runs is modified, changed and re-modified several times before it hopefully becomes more successful. But if you can build your business on strong foundations, the future is much more certain and the overall likelihood of the business doing well is greatly increased. It doesn't guarantee it but it becomes less risky.

This doesn't mean that if you have been running your business for a while and the foundations are not strong you are doomed - in fact far from it. What it means is that for long-term success and your peace of mind, you have the opportunity to go back and do some work on your business foundations to dramatically strengthen them. From my own experience, this means tidying up a lot of issues that have been lingering or ignored for many years.

The topics covered in this section are:

- Making your business bigger than one person
- Write a Business Plan - or get someone to write one for you
- Understanding the importance of systems
- Understanding finances - taking control of your business
- Keeping good records always pays off in the long run.

Making your business bigger than one person

Most businesses have a product champion, key person, hero or some other similar kind of person. There are various arguments for the 'inspirational' type of leader or a 'nuts and bolts' kind of person, but that's for a blog or a social media forum somewhere.

Put simply this means that one person is driving the machine and it's their passion that propels the business forward. In the early stages of a business, this is very normal and a natural starting point. That is why there are so many people running their own small business.

But for a business to grow and have longevity it really needs to be bigger than one person.

Now when I say this I don't mean you need to have more than one person involved, I mean the business needs to appear more like a business than an individual.
If you don't build your business in this manner the end result can be that the product or service champion is left a battered and broken wreck by the side of the entrepreneurial roadside.

Let's use a mechanic as an example - Bill Smith is an excellent mechanic. He starts his own workshop called 'Bill Smith's Really Excellent Garage'. Before long the customers are streaming in, asking for Bill Smith. He does the job and they are very happy.

They keep coming back, and they tell all of their friends. Bill Smith gets busier and busier but a strange thing starts to happen. As he employs mechanics to help him out, his customers make it clear they only want him to work on their car because he always does such a good job.
No matter how much he protests and sells the skills of his employees his customers are adamant. Bill Smith ends up working more and more hours to meet his customers' expectations.

He has no time to focus on the running of his business or his life outside of the business and slowly his world starts to fall apart. Bill Smith ends up burnt out and exhausted. His business is in a mess and his customers leave in droves. Clearly, a sad story that started out much nicer than it ended.

Unfortunately, it is a common story. Of course, the biggest irony is that this generally only happens to people who are very good at what they do.

If Bill Smith had set his business up as 'The Really Excellent Garage', where Bill was the owner but he had a team of 'really excellent mechanics', his clients would have had a very different perception. They no longer had to deal with the main man; they simply had to deal with one of the 'really excellent mechanics'.

This is a shift in perception that enables the business to grow without being so dependent on the one person.

If you are happy to build your business to a size that is manageable by one person and you have the ability to say no to customers, your business doesn't need to be bigger than one person. But if you have aspirations of building and one day selling your business, it is a really good idea to make it bigger than one person as soon as you can.

I personally have a business coach. A genuinely nice bloke. Now he has lots of clients, writes books, writes blogs, does day-long workshops and presentations, videos, podcasts and TV appearances.

Where does he find the time?

His PA. She's not a 'Timelord', (that's the one Dr Who reference in the book), and she hasn't got a DeLorean, but she buys him time. Now she may not appreciate me saying this, but she does all the liaising with the accountants, hotels, meeting room organisers and diary commanders. She does venue bookings. She manages his diary. She even tells him when he's having some time off. In effect, she does the boring stuff. Simply because as a business if these 'uninspiring tasks' aren't done, my coach, who is the 'face of the business', can't-do his stuff. There just simply aren't enough hours in the day.

So how do you make your business bigger than one person? Think about the name of the business.
As much as it can be a good idea to use your name to get the business going it can end up being a liability. Let your customers deal with other people in the business, and make sure you talk up the other people.

Show your customers that you are a team. Even if it is a small team, it is a team nevertheless and their needs will be met equally by anyone who is a part of that team.

Make sure your business has a strong corporate image so the customer expects there to be other people involved. Most importantly, let go of the reins a little and let the people you work with step up to the plate. You may be surprised at the results.

Write a Business Plan or Get Someone to Do it for You.

It's easy for a business to blunder along under its own steam and momentum, not really having any significant direction or plan. These kinds of businesses are a worry. The best comparison I have is that it is like driving around without your headlights on at night. You can kind of make out the shapes on the road, and you will probably be able to miss most of the hazards, but eventually you're going to hit something—odds on, it will hurt.......a lot. A Business Plan is the headlights of the business. It gives you direction and focus and in many ways it is a map to guide you forward.

Getting a Business Plan done is not a cheap exercise, nor should it be. It is a significant document for any business and you tend to get what you pay for. You can buy a host of books that will tell you how to write your own Business Plan and personally I am an advocate of you writing your own. It's your 'baby' and providing you do it objectively you'll 'own' the business plan'.

Don't make it too long though. If it's not quick and easy to read, it'll end up gathering dust somewhere or propping up a coffee table.

The key elements should contain:

- Who are you?
- What do you do?

- Why are you doing it?
- Who are your main competitors, with listed strengths and weaknesses?
- What are your strengths and weaknesses?
- How much do you need to start up with?
- How much will you make?
- When are things going to happen and who are going to do them?

Anything more than that and it'll look like a copy of 'War and Peace'.

What can you do today?

Think about what you need to do to make your business bigger than one person. Is it a matter of changing your business name or starting to raise the profile of the other people working with you?

If you are not sure ask your staff, your customers or your business mentors and associates.

Letting go is often the hardest part of this process and something that I've been accused of in the past. I'd like to think it's a perfection thing, but in reality, it's a control freak thing.

Write a business plan and 'own it'. I sat down a hundred times to write my own Business Plan and I never got past the title page. I am too close. I then paid a reputable company to write one for me and it is excellent. They identified issues and made recommendations that I would never have even thought of, let alone realised, as potential hazards or opportunities.

My business has a clear direction and focus and every week I sit down and review my Business Plan to make sure I am on track to achieve what I want to.

Understanding the importance of systems.

Systems are all the talk of the business world these days and have been ever since a very smart man called Michael Gerber wrote the very famous book The E myth. He wasn't the first person to come up with the idea of systems, they have been around for thousands of years, but he was one of the first people to be able to describe how important they are for the long-term success and sustainability of a business. Especially if you want to scale it and grow it. The concept of systems is simply to add structure to the day-to-day processes that happen within a business. McDonald's is the easiest business to use as an example here.

The entire organisation is built on systems from the bottom up to the very top. Systems mean there is a very clear procedure to follow to do anything within a business. At McDonald's there is a system or a checklist for pre-opening in the morning, for getting the kitchen started, for greeting the customers, for making the burgers, for putting the food on the tray, for thanking the customer and for cleaning up after the customer. Anyone can learn a specific system within a matter of minutes. This makes training easy and it means a very high level of consistency in the business - and customers love consistency. Let's be fair, you can get a McBurger in Lands End and in John-o-Groats and it should taste the same. (There are worldwide variations and in some cases, they have better menus, but I'll let that go for now. You hear me, Ronald McDonald? Sort it out!)

Back to systems. Systems can be applied to virtually every business at some level. The biggest problem is that most entrepreneurs are too busy running or being 'in' their business to document the systems they use and they tend to be kept in their heads. The hard bit is getting it onto paper and making sure they are reviewed regularly. If you just try to replicate without these processes down, the end result is generally barely controlled chaos and inconsistent service - which customers hate.

Systemised businesses are very popular. They are appealing to people buying businesses because they can be managed much easier than non-systemised businesses. That is why franchises are so popular. (Think McDonald's, think Subway.) You get a manual that tells you exactly what to do and when to do it.

Systems are golden dynamite. They let you get on with running the business. They are cost conscious because staff can learn their jobs quickly. They provide a mechanism for giving your customers consistent service. They make your business more appealing to buy. There really are no downsides to putting systems in place.

What can you do today?

If you haven't read The E-Myth by Michael Gerber, go out and grab a copy today. If you read it a while ago, pull it off the shelf, dust it down and read it again. If it is already by your bed and you have read it recently compile a list of the processes that happen within your business that could be systemised and start doing it. Get your staff involved - often they have a much better idea about how to systemise a business process because they do it all day every day.

Understanding finances- taking control of your business.

If you are like me the financial aspect of running the business is a chore. It is much more interesting and enjoyable to be at the business end - doing what you do. I would much rather be developing a new marketing campaign or discussing future plans with a client than talking margins and profit and loss or cash flow with my accountant. But this can be a little dangerous. If you don't pay enough attention to your business' finances it is very easy to get into a lot of trouble, often before you even realise you are in trouble.

As a business owner and as an entrepreneur the buck stops with you. Not knowing or not understanding your financial position is not a good argument during a tax audit (and if you haven't experienced one of them, boy...are you in for a treat).

I strongly recommend two things. Firstly, from now on question your accountant or book-keeper about what everything in your business' financial means and what it's for. Secondly, know your numbers when it comes to trying to achieve. If you're setting yourself financial targets whether its sales or costs, you need to know how close, or how far away you are from it.

Keeping good records always pays off in the long run

I remember my first visit to an accountant. I had three years' worth of business records crammed into three shoe boxes. My poor accountant. Her face was a picture. Her language not so pretty...

Since then I have well and truly learned the lesson of keeping good records.

Quite simply not keeping good records will cost you money, often a lot of money. Basically, there are two lots of records that need to be kept in business-money in and money out. Poor records regarding money coming into the business tend to border on tax evasion or at least avoidance, and taxation departments in all countries tend to be rather down on this subject. (More so small businesses, but that's my own opinion of course.)

Poor record keeping of money going out of the business often means you can't claim justified expenses because you don't have the appropriate receipts or records. So not only do you not get the deduction, the expense is classed as a personal expense and you have to pay tax on it. Whichever way you look at it, poor record keeping does not do a lot towards building a successful business.

What can you do today?

If you don't understand what your business' financial statements actually mean, make an appointment to get your accountant to explain them to you - it is well worth the expense. Then book yourself in to do a basic bookkeeping course.

Often records can be in such a mess it is hard to know where to start and that very problem prevents the entrepreneur from getting their act together. The best thing to do is to bite the bullet and get someone in to help you. Get a professional; odds on they have been through this situation before (and you should check to make sure they have). Generally, you will find they can rattle off half a dozen stories of businesses that have been in far worse condition than yours, which really does make you feel a lot better.

Even if you think your records are pretty good, maybe today is a good day to review your systems and record keeping looking for ways to make it even better.
Look at bank statements no matter how silly you may feel. Get to know the terminology and decide whether you agree your books accurately reflect your business. It really isn't that complicated.

From my experience, many accountants aren't that good at communicating so they don't tend to give you good descriptions. In all fairness, they deal with the terms day in day out, so most are second nature to them and perhaps they forget they aren't second nature to us.
Make it your business to understand your accounts.

The second recommendation I would make is to enrol in a simple business bookkeeping course, online preferably, so you get to know more about the processes being used in your own business. I am not saying you should do your own bookwork if you don't want to, but at least understand it better. It is very liberating to be able to look at a profit and loss statement and understand what it means. Most people have no idea.If you think it is time to dig out the shoe boxes and call an accountant, do it.

Get the phone book out, search engine search it or ask your business associates and mentors for a recommendation.

Take control of your record keeping today. If you think your records are pretty smart, try to find at least one thing you could be doing to improve it.

CHAPTER 5

CUSTOMERS ARE THE MOST IMPORTANT PEOPLE ON YOUR PAYROLL

Winning businesses understand the importance of keeping their customers happy. They know they have to exceed their expectations whenever they can, let alone meet them. They have to respect their customers and they have to be better than their competitors at delivering high levels of customer service.

Customer service is a huge issue and one that is not easy to cover in one section of a book like this, which is aiming to deliver a well-rounded overview of building a successful business. But the topics covered in this section are the most important issues to consider.

In this section we'll cover:

- It's all about respect - if you don't respect your customers don't expect them to come back
- Never lose touch with your customers
- Do you over promise and under deliver?
- The first 30 seconds
- Talk about customer service to your staff - a lot
- Reward good customers
- Keep a notepad in your pocket

- Time - the one commodity that causes the most grief
- Customer expectations are changing - we all need to change with them
- Look at the entire customer service picture - not just little pieces
- Who is your biggest competitor?

It's all about respect - if you don't respect your customers don't expect them to come back.

It is hard to build a winning business if you don't respect your customers (mind you plenty of businesses seem to have a good go at it). Respect is a very powerful word when it comes to customers and there are a lot of ways to show respect for your customers. Often though, it is easier to come up with examples of how customers are treated with little or no respect.

What do I mean by respecting your customers?

I think there are a number of areas where you can show respect for your customers including:

- Respect their time - they shouldn't have to wait for you. Making someone wait in a queue for half an hour is not a sign of respect
- Respect the fact that they made a conscious decision to use your business
- Respect the fact that their opinions regarding your business are important and appreciated
- Respect the fact that if they refer someone else to your business they are showing a significant sign of commitment to your business

- Respect the fact that if you fail to meet their expectations they will take their business elsewhere.

Respect for customers has to start at the top. If the people that own the business don't respect their customers it is impossible to expect the staff down the line to show any respect for customers. We all need to have a very clear 'customer commitment statement'. This is very simply a one or two sentence description that captures the essence of your philosophy towards your customers. Anyone involved in your business should be made aware of your customer commitment statement, including your customers.

Never lose touch with your customers.

Sir Richard Branson has a well-told story that no-one is entirely certain whether it happened or not. If it did, it certainly shows his drive to be better at customer service than his rivals and shows how he likes to keep in touch with what his customers want.

The story goes that he read a tweet from an unhappy train customer. The customer was sat on the toilet at the time and tweeted there was no toilet roll. He saw the tweet and made sure a member of the team was at the next station with a toilet roll.

Not entirely sure what happened next, but you got to give credit for a service delivery and it shows that he still takes an active interest in his customers.

Another example would be when TESCO's under the leadership of Sir Terry Leahy became a retailing giant. When he picked up the reigns at the start of his tenure, according to his book, '10 Rules of Management', TESCO Supermarkets were struggling. They had forgotten a key component of their business. And Sir Terry was the man to remember it and then used that very component to set the sector alight.

He turned it around by using the views of the customer to turn TESCO from a struggling chain into a retail behemoth.

A lot of business people could learn valuable lessons from these examples. But are they really willing to see the customer for what they are? They are the lifeblood of the business. The most important people on the payroll.

What can you do today?

Make up your own customer commitment statement and make certain everyone involved in your business and your customers know what it is.

Personally, I believe that anyone who sits on the board of a large company should spend a prerequisite amount of time dealing with customers at the coal face of the business. Too often large companies lose touch with their customers simply because the people making the decisions are too sheltered from the front line. (Having worked in large retail organisations the customer is often forgotten. When area or district managers are due to visit, overtime is chucked about all over the place to make the store look nice. To make it look like it should. The problem created by doing that regularly meant that the systems and processes that were put in place to improve productivity and product availability were being made to look better than they really were. As soon as the 'visit' was done, all the shop floor staff were sent home and there was no-one to serve the customers! Therefore these more traditional retailers were forgetting who their most important person was...the customer!)

In small businesses we often spend a lot of our time trying to get away from directly dealing with customers because it can be tough, demanding, frustrating and time-consuming. I am certainly not saying that every business owner should spend forty hours a week behind the till, but I do believe every one of them should be communicating with the customers on a regular basis. Depending on the type of business, this may mean making a few phone calls each week, or it may mean physically standing on the shop floor. From my experience, those businesses where the final decision maker interacts directly with customers on a regular basis tend to offer far greater levels of customer service than those that do not. Don't be afraid to talk to your customers and to ask for their opinions - remember without customers your business would be a very lonely place. And bust.

Do you over promise and under deliver?

In businesses that are overly busy this point poses a challenge. In businesses not so busy, it is unforgivable. Over promising and under delivering is the best way to lose customers as it breaks every customer service rule. Firstly you are building up the customer's expectations, probably higher than they were initially, then you not only fail to meet their expectations, you fail miserably.

It is easy to get pressured into over promising and under delivering. In the business coaching and strategy industry, it seems when people do want advice, they want strategies quickly that contain the mythical 'silver bullet', but the reality is they take time to prepare. A rushed strategy can be flawed and the end results disastrous for the business concerned. I specifically explain this to my clients at length and I have to be careful to make sure the timeframe I quote to deliver their strategy is realistic and achievable. Once committed, I will move heaven and earth to make sure the very best quality product is delivered on time.

I'll give you an example of how a trip of mine can be used as an example of 'managing expectations' when it comes to customer service. This is from a blog I wrote in 2015, called 'Customer Service – Stains, Rudeness, Superheroes and the little stuff.'

"It's Sunday lunchtime as I sit on the balcony overlooking Paris. I can see for miles. I can see the Eiffel Tower, which reminds me always of Blackpool. I can see the Louvre. I can see Notre-Dame. I can even see further afield thanks to the telescope our kind host left behind.

I have had a wonderful experience, but I've also had some of the worst customer experiences in my life…and not all in France!

My journey started in the mighty Luton. The home of Luton Town football club and the famous son that is Nick Owen, once of Good Morning Britain and now of BBC Midlands News. We chose to stay there the night before flying out because our flight was at 6 am and I'm really quite a grumpy so and so if I don't get enough sleep.
We're flying with 'x'. Now some like 'x'. Some don't. Up until I write this, all I can say are favourable things about them. Quick, cheap, prompt and great service when on the plane. xHotel? Oh dear God, no!!!!

Here is the review I left on 'trip advisor' about our 8hr stay at the Luton xHotel:

" 'Stains Cum To Luton'

To make things perfectly clear, we love x. We hate xHotel Luton. As the title suggests, may we congratulate one of the previous occupants for getting his juices that far up the blackout blind, (but not that difficult considering the bed is right underneath the damn thing)! May we also congratulate staff on the homely smell of urine by the lift area, which helped us imagine the feeling of homelessness shared by some of the people hanging around outside. And finally thanks to the prostitute we met leaving as we left at 4 am for our flight, in reminding us and anyone that visits this area, that it would probably be best to travel a few miles further for a better looking and younger extracurricular activity."

I should have also gone on to discuss the port-a-loo style toilet and shower area, which meant that you could actually have a shower whilst sat on the toilet. The scrubbing of a few more stains on the orange colouring of the 'x' logo and the fact that their 4:3 TV (remember those?), no longer worked. Add the one pillow. The one sheet. And the goodbye grunt we received as we left in the morning from the staff as said prostitute was chatting them up, all in all, was probably the worst hotel experience ever.

After our near argument with a security official at Luton airport, (who knew that Luton were more anal on toiletries than a far bigger, more efficient and entirely more professional airport such as Gatwick?), we had an uneventful flight and arrival at Charles-de-Gaulle. We then made our way to the French Train system…and this is where our real, genuine, first taste of French customer service was served up.

We knew where we were going, we just needed to purchase a ticket.

(Quick tip. The fastest way to buy one is via the ticket machines using debit cards...not using the cash we had taken the trouble of exchanging into Euro's.) So we queued as all good British people do at the ticket desk.
There were three windows open. Two seemed to have the nicest and most helpful people there. Showing people where they needed to go on their various maps. Explaining what the best ticket was, all in French style English.
We, however, got the one person in the place that really couldn't have given a flying monkey about anyone. I watched her as several people before us had approached. If she didn't understand them she shooed them away with what can only be described as 'pantomime aggression'.
She kept leaning back in her chair and making comments to someone that was behind the scenes and laughing.
We approached her as any prey would do a hungry bear. We politely pointed at where we wanted to go on the map and asked for the number of tickets. She promptly shoved another map through the feeding hole of the desk. Pointed at the screen and grunted.

It was going well.

We handed over our hard earned cash. She leant back, still not actually having looked at us so far, chatted to someone, then rocked forward like a ravenous wild bear in for the kill, snatching the tickets from her beaten up machine, thrusting the tickets out of the hole.

As they shot out onto our side we realised that not only could she not smile, be polite, or have any redeeming quality whatsoever, we also realised she also couldn't count. She'd sold us an extra ticket that we really didn't need. But as we'd been up since 3 am already, we Britishly took the tickets and I moaned my head off about her utter ignorance and the French education system that meant she counted three when two were only needed.

There is a stereotype which does it rounds when it comes to the French, in the same way, there is about the British, and this person had done nothing if not justify it.

What she had done was give the train company a poor image at the start of the customer 'experience'. A customer experience starts when a customer chooses an avenue to interact with your company. When it came to this situation, we chose to speak to a human being. The human being was rude and genuinely unhelpful. Whether it is the first point of contact on website, LinkedIn, Facebook, Twitter, Phone or in person, first impressions count. Many companies would have lost a sale at this point, but as its national transport, there was little we could do. There were also people wandering around with machine guns; so best keep quiet eh?

But look at the interaction we got at the hotel and then at the airport. Just one person on each occasion. Just one interaction and our opinions had been coloured. For the hotel, we wanted somewhere, clean, tidy and hospitable. The airport colleague...just plain, bloody rude. Yes, members of the public can be rude back, but in this scenario, we were not. We were polite if not slightly overwhelmed with the vast queues of people making a whole lot of noise around us. So when people don't pay attention to what they say or what they do, it can have a lasting effect on those customers that it involves.

However, I also want to share the two utterly brilliant experiences in an art gallery and where we were staying, both in Paris.

I want to tell you about an amazing art gallery, Galerie Sakura, in the Bercy Village part of Paris. I have an 11-year-old son, called Kieran that is a) Lego mad and b) Superhero mad. Combine the pair and I should own shares in the Danish company. However, I stumbled upon it and it was showing works of art depicting superheroes in many unique and exciting ways. The prices were reasonable, but I could have quite honestly spent a year's profit in there and bought everything, turning my house into a gallery of its own. There was a fairly strict no photo policy, but there was a book on offer of one of the artists and it came with a price tag of €40 (about £30). Now I certainly don't spend that on books normally, but I really wanted to take home the memories of the work and show my son. I asked the lady behind the desk for a copy and she immediately wanted to speak English to me.

Looking back on the conversation, she actually used F.O.R.M. on me. (Family, Occupation, Recreation, and Message). Not only did she seem interested in where I was from and who I was buying the book for, she slipped in several messages about the pictures I had been looking at. It wasn't a hard sell. It was relationship selling. She took my details for a mailing list. She took time to give me her business card and details of the galleries website.
It was a genuinely, nice and relaxed sales experience. It wasn't anything out of this world, but, it was a relationship building experience. I could buy from her again. I could make a purchase and have it shipped out, (she had mentioned that was possible), and it all seemed no trouble to her. So because she had been sincere in getting to know who was buying, to her a fairly inexpensive item amongst

items that could reach hundreds, I most certainly would buy from her again.

And when it comes to experiences, I have to certainly commend the owner of the apartment we stayed in, Olivier. As someone who spends his time working in another part of the world, he helped make the Paris experience superb. Not only was he in regular touch up to our arrival, but was easily contactable during our stay.

He arranges for his cleaner, Fazia, to meet his guests on arrival. She takes time to tell us about the keys, where everything is in the flat, provides us with mobile phones whilst in the country, home phone, Internet, free bicycle passes, maps, places to eat, places to drink, see and experience. They leave these bits of information in a useful pack in the apartment so we can refer to them at any time. There's even a section, called "If things go wrong and how to fix them easily."

This is a great example of how to under promise, but over deliver.

All we did was book an apartment for our stay through an app. All we wanted was somewhere fairly central so we could get to where we were going and do what we needed to do and be able to have a decent night's sleep.
What we got was all of the above but an experience that someone had taken time to improve, by thinking of the little things and delivering them.

He left us two mobile phones with unlimited plans so we could use the map software, costing us less than our own fee incurring mobile phones in Europe. Knowing who to call in the event of a leak or a problem. Being able to research places of interest on the free Wi-Fi. Being able to go to quality and highly recommended restaurants, bars and markets without the fear of being ripped off. And the best bit? If you were visiting for a holiday, all the metro and bus route information to help you to get to the iconic places in and around Paris, as well what you were likely to pay. It was a better version of trip advisor, by someone who cared enough to think of it in the first place.

And here's the positive relationship, customer experience, silver bullet…..I've recommended this apartment to people already. The view itself was outstanding. The outside of the apartment left a lot to be desired. But the apartment itself and the experience the host managed to deliver us from of all places, Israel, is something that many businesses should pay attention to. I genuinely believe my stay in Paris would have felt and remembered very differently had my good experiences not been so positive.

Take away these two things… Relationships build sales. And under promising and over delivering generates goodwill and referrals. It's not 'rocket science', but it's amazing what happens when you or members of your team don't buy into that.

What can you do today?

Consider how you can spend more time with customers to get their feedback and opinions on what your business is doing well and what it could do better. It is better to set a realistic timeframe, one you can achieve, than one you can't possibly achieve, which is guaranteed to end in tears for all the parties concerned.

There are of course many other forms of overpromising and under delivering.

One of the most obvious is food. We have all seen sensational television advertisements promoting mouth-watering meals, filling us with expectation, only to find the end product is a shrivelled, poor impersonation of what was in the commercial. Likewise, the advertisement may spout on about how your business is valued and how staff will treat you like celebrities, but when you pick up the phone the person on the other end treats you like anything but royalty.

Some of this problem is due to the distance between the marketing people and the end product. But as someone who understands marketing, I have never seen a brief that said: "Make sure you show our burgers looking soggy and unappetising". The key here is to be honest in your representation of your product or service.
Over promise and under deliver - don't underestimate the customer's intelligence. They know when they are being treated with contempt and they will soon let you know.

The first 30 seconds.

The first 30 seconds of any business interaction are best considered an interview.

A customer forms a lot of opinions in this initial window of opportunity for you. Generally most impressions are done subconsciously with a simple end result being a message from the brain of the customer saying, 'I will come back here again' or, 'I will not come back here again'. Sure this process may take longer in some businesses, but you get the point.

I do a lot of mystery shopper evaluations for various businesses. This is where I visit the business or contact the business as a customer but my job is to evaluate how they could do things better, generally from a customer service perspective. My most common negative comment is that the business fails to impress from the start and that sets the mood for the rest of the interaction.

Make your first business impressions count. If you have a business where people come in off the street, you always need to look impressive, neat, tidy and ready to go.

You'll also find that in the world of technology, you may not even get the first 30 seconds. So many businesses are reviewed on websites, review sites and on social media, that Google themselves are starting to call the online version of decision making, 'Decision 0'.

People buy from people; they don't buy things unless they absolutely need them. If you look at all materialistic things like phones, iPad's, laptops, cars, TVs and things like that, they buy them because someone, (usually an early adopter), sings their praises or the sales person does a really good job.

Think about it. Is buying a brand new car a sensible decision?

No!

As soon as you drive it off the forecourt it's losing money. There are pound notes streaming out of the exhaust, so why do people buy brand new cars?

It's a psychology thing. People want status objects. People want things that other people have got. If you listen to the patter the sales person has, invariably they have a story or stories of someone that bought that model, for the same purpose as you, in the same circumstances as you.

Yes it's probably bullshit, but the sales person is doing a great job at tugging on the emotional side of your brain. Same as washing machine sales people, phone sales people, insurance sales people and other aspects of sales that people have low regard for. Hearing or seeing stories about people making purchases or having certain experiences makes decisions for people.

So 'social proof' or reviews can be a huge influencer in whether someone does business with you.

"Social proof, also known as informational social influence, is a psychological phenomenon where people assume the actions of others in an attempt to reflect correct behaviour for a given situation."
Source: Wikipedia

One of the biggest questions that seems to be recurring and a flashing light on whether you're customer service is really working is how you deal with 'Bad Reviews'.

First off do not ignore it!!!

Second thing to do is to contact them PRIVATELY and try to resolve any issues. It is not a cool thing to do to argue with them about what the issues are.

I have seen an argument develop on a Facebook advert and it was hilarious. A marketing professional posted and boosted a Facebook post. It was advertising an event of some kind about getting on page one of Google, (that old chestnut). Another professional took offence at the post and placed a comment on the post. The poster then replied in an argumentative way and it went back and forth. Meanwhile this post is doing its rounds on several thousand people's timelines and it has to be said showing neither in a good light!

Thirdly, should anything slanderous or defamatory be out there, refer them to the website owner or social media administrators. I do however want to share with you a funny reply to a poor review of a restaurant. You can't help but smile, but I don't want you doing this unless you are in fact a comedian.

" Cafe52, Owner at Cafe 52, responded to this review, April28, 2015.

Oddly enough I was waiting for this remarkably creative piece of writing from either you or another of your 'party'. You either have a twisted sense of reality or you're simply full of it. But let me clarify the actual situation for the curious readers:

1. Your colleague's leg suffered a ½ inch scratch from a broken glass that hit the floor. It's not unusual for a member of the waiting staff to drop something in the hospitality industry (Wait till they start wearing roller skates!)
2. Your colleague was tended to immediately and a drum of antiseptic wipes (contents 200) were put on the table and several wipes (better safe than sorry!) were used to treat the wound. Thereafter a clean dry towel with crushed ice was put around the leg of the alleged victim (just in case the leg swelled up to the size of Saturn, resulting in a lunar explosion).
3. The alleged victim was offered a choice of plasters , however we were out of 'Does this plaster match my outfit' variety, so it was either skin coloured plasters or those bright blue ones. The skin toned plaster seemed to do the job.

4. I; yes me, made regular appearances at your table to make sure the leg wasn't going to drop off and there wasn't a sea of blood flooding down the middle of the restaurant and to check if you were enjoying your meal given that your collective faces were smiling from ear to ear I took that as a yes.
5. All is well.
6. I revisited your table about 15 minutes before you were due to leave and the vino had made its bed in your head. At which point you started feeling my backside.

And that's how it went."

What can you do today?

Evaluate your business - are there areas where you over promise and under deliver? Why not make a commitment to end this cycle today?

You and your staff need to be well presented and the 'welcome' needs to be honest and sincere. If your business is one where people phone in, the call needs to be answered promptly, and the person answering the call needs to speak clearly and listen to what the caller is saying. They need to be able to answer the queries or direct the caller to someone who can help them (not just put them in a never-ending cycle of 'someone else's problem'). If your business' first point of contact is through a brochure in the mail it needs to get the reader's attention quickly and answer the right questions. If the reader has to try and figure out what it is all about, it will end up in the too hard basket or the bin.

If your first point of contact is your website, then it needs to be easy to read, easy to navigate, mobile friendly, be able to contact you or the company within an agreed service time.

Can they call you from the website?
Can they buy, book or ask for a quote online?

Remember first impressions set the mood for all future interactions and dealings. Make your first 30 seconds as good as they can be and your business will be well and truly on the way to achieving winning status.

Talk about customer service to your team - a lot.

Customer service is an issue that many businesses really struggle to get a handle on. For some people, it is simply serving customers quickly and politely, but in reality, it goes much deeper.

Earlier in this chapter, I talked about the importance of respecting your customers, which I genuinely believe is the starting point when it comes to delivering high levels of customer service.

While you may respect your customers, the relevance of this is often hard to pass on to your team.

Most businesses will talk endlessly about sales to staff: is the business reaching its targets, how can sales be improved, how can more customers be attracted and how can they be encouraged to spend more with the business?

The topic of customer service is often overlooked, generally, because I feel that business owners aren't really sure how to address more than a few very obvious customer service issues.

Customer service should be talked about a lot. It should be debated, it should be reviewed and it should be discussed at every opportunity. This can get a little boring and start to sound like a broken record so it is up to the person doing the talking to be a little innovative.

What can you do today?

Review your own first 30 seconds.

Make a list of five things you could do right now to change your initial contact with a customer from mediocre to magnificent and implement them today. Attention to detail is important here.

Buy a book on customer service with lots of great ideas on how to stand out from the crowd by offering exceptional customer service. There are many books available and most contain excellent tips.

Encourage your staff to make suggestions on how they feel your business' customer service could be improved. Ask your customers for their feedback and recommendations. Talk about these recommendations with your team and see if they can be implemented. By getting your staff and customers involved the concept of customer service becomes much more tangible.

In short, devote as much time to improving customer service as you do to improving sales and your business will grow naturally as it gains a reputation for offering excellent service.

Reward good customers

Are you forgetting the one group of people that have already made your business into what is today?

Good customers are hard to find and there are plenty of other businesses fighting for them. For this reason, it is essential you reward good customers for coming back to your business. There are many ways to show you appreciate your regular customers and most businesses can easily implement either a formal or informal system that will do exactly that.

A formal reward system may be a loyalty card style of programme, where repeat customers receive discounts or special offers whenever they use the business. It may include invitations to special events, access to special products or services or a special incentive after making a certain number of purchases.

Businesses that have really got a handle on their marketing are the businesses that have an email strategy in place. This way they can keep in touch with their current customers AND attract new ones through the various sign-up methods.

An informal system could be something more spur of the moment, where you offer a 'reward' on the spot to a regular customer as your way of saying thank you for their business. My local coffee shop does this very well. Every once in a while the owner will refuse to take my money, saying, 'This one is on the house'.
A very nice touch that is most appreciated and, of course, I keep going back for more. I don't expect the freebie but I certainly appreciate it. I just wish more pubs would do it...I

think some of them have had a fair share out of me in 41 years.

What can you do today?

Go out today and buy a book on customer service and start to introduce the recommendations to your staff. Don't bombard them with 100 ideas in one hit - introduce one or two at a time and then action them properly.

Are you rewarding your regular customers or are you taking them for granted and simply assuming that they will keep coming back?

Why not implement either a formal or an informal rewards system for your good customers today?

Today, do something amazing for your existing or longest customers - go on, delight them!

Keep a notepad in your pocket.

Successful business entrepreneurs and owners tend to be very good observers. They have a thirst for knowledge and they are always looking for ways to make their business run better. Whenever they deal with another business they are often evaluating the service they are getting and looking for ideas they can use. The hard part can be remembering all of the good things observed.

As a budding entrepreneur and business owner of the next big thing, (see how confident in you I am?), you need to become an observer. Every interaction could possibly contain some valuable idea that you could use to make your business more profitable. However, it is easy to forget your observations in the course of a busy day.

If you keep a notepad handy you'll find it takes only a second to jot down a couple of notes for later reference. I do this a lot and subsequently, I have notepads all over the place - in my car, on my bedside table, around the house, in my man bag - I always carry one with me. This may be a bit of overkill for some, but I have so many things going around in my mind that if I don't write things down it is easy for me to forget them.

I find that when I'm driving, especially long distances, I have this amazing influx of good ideas and I need to write them down then and there. Of course, this means I am forever pulling over to write notes, but it doesn't bother me for a second because, by the time I arrive at my destination, I have a pile of new inspirational ideas that can be used in my business or by my clients to make their businesses more profitable.

I have friends who keep small tape recorders in their pockets for the same reason (at least that's what they tell me). Whenever they have a thought they simply pull out the recorder and tape a message to themselves. Many mobile phones have this capacity as well, but the amount of recording time on them is quite limited at present.
To make your business as successful as it can be, be prepared to become an observer of every other business you deal with, from the local news agency to your bank. Look out for good ideas that you can use in your business.

What can you do today?

Buy yourself some notepads and leave them in readily accessible spots.

Alternatively, buy yourself a mini recorder. Start to become an observer.

Time - the one commodity that causes the most grief.

The one topic sure to spark unanimous agreement in the modern business world is that we are all struggling to find enough time to get everything we need to get done. There are so many different aspects of our lives that demand our time and attention. Often it can all be a little overwhelming. Time - the greatest commodity which, ironically, we all have the same amount of.

When you look at time from a customer service perspective it is the one area where consumers are unforgiving. If a business wastes their time - look out.

Winning businesses realise this and they will do their utmost to make sure their customers' time is treated as the precious commodity it is.

Think about your own frustrations when it comes to time - related customer service issues. Waiting for too long in a restaurant, standing in queues anywhere, waiting around at home for a tradesperson to turn up and make a repair, waiting for someone to call you back and a myriad of other typically time frustrating scenarios.

Think of how your mind processes thoughts regarding certain businesses. For example, you might have a favourite coffee shop but you know you have to wait quite a long time for a coffee. Often this will stop you from going there simply because you haven't got the time to stand around waiting for a coffee. After a while, you stop going there and so do lots of other people. Sure the business may do well initially, but eventually, the owners will wonder where all of the customers have gone.

If you can show your customers that you respect their time they will appreciate it, even if you don't always get it right. Most businesses have peaks and troughs when they are busier than usual or quieter than usual, and customers understand this. Most of us eat at restaurants for either lunch or dinner, along with everyone else. So these are the times when you expect to wait a little longer. But when the restaurant is quiet, we expect to be served fast and efficiently.

One of the biggest mistakes I observe with businesses that fail to respect time is that they don't acknowledge the customers who are waiting. No eye contact or recognition is made until the customer is the next one at the counter. So much grief can be overcome by simply smiling at the people waiting and letting them know the wait won't be long. Acknowledge the customer and show them you understand their time is valuable and you are doing your best to serve them quickly.

It all comes back to communication. If you are going to be late, call the customer. If you can't deliver a product on time, let them know.

Look for ways to streamline what you do to speed up the customer service.
Often it is the little things that can make businesses serve their customers faster.

It might be the layout of the business if it is a retail style of operation. It might be staffing levels at critical times or it might be the actual sales process itself - maybe it is overly complicated and has too much paperwork. Maybe your team need to be better trained.
Regardless of the business, find ways to serve your customers as fast as possible and your business will

develop a reputation for providing excellent service and more customers will use it.

What can you do today?

Look at the way you serve your customers.

Is there any part of the sales process where you could show a greater level of respect for your customers' time by speeding up the system?

Look at how other businesses serve their customers and see if you can adopt any of their procedures in your business to speed up your customer service.

Today, implement one action that will make a difference and enjoy the difference it makes.

Customer expectations are changing - we all need to change with them.

I am an advocate of the importance of improving customer service and the easiest way to do this is to exceed your customers' expectations. The difficult part is that customer expectations are constantly changing and that can make it hard to know where you stand.

There was a time when customer expectations didn't really matter because there were not a lot of options for them to choose from. Cars came in one or two colours, so did a suit. Restaurant menus had a handful of choices. When you went to the cinema there was only one movie playing or there was only one channel to watch on the television or listen to on the radio. Those times have well and truly passed.

Choice is one commodity that is certainly not in short supply and everyone wants to succeed by attracting more customers than their opposition. Added to this is the fact that we all have access to far more media than ever before - magazines, newspapers, the internet, television, radio and a host of other forms of communications - all of them bombarding consumers with marketing and advertising messages. It is well documented that this is the driving force in consumer trends and every advertising agency and marketing professional is trying to find a way to get their product in front of more potential customers.
So we, the consumer, are well informed, aware and intelligent, and we have high expectations that are changing constantly.

What does this mean to the average business owner and entrepreneur?

It means we can never sit back and be complacent when it comes to meeting our customers' expectations. What works today may not work tomorrow, we need to always be one step ahead of the pack and we need to become better at communicating with our customers. But most importantly, we need to be able to adapt the way we do business to meet these changing expectations.

The age of 'that is the way we always did it' is long gone and the dinosaurs still living in that Jurassic mindset are finding out fast that it is not a sustainable business model. I see a lot more companies failing today after decades of being successful, mostly because they can't change with the times and their customers outgrow them.

Look at the entire customer service picture - not just little pieces

Many businesses consider customer service as just the time they are dealing face-to-face with their customers. In reality, the entire customer service picture is much bigger. It is often easy to go into a business where the initial greeting from someone behind the counter is excellent, and then everything else that follows falls apart.

I noticed this recently at a huge DIY store that I visited. I was met at the front door by a delightful young lady who sincerely welcomed me to the business and advised me where to go to find what I needed. What a great start.

So I trundled off to find the various bits of hardware, which meant nothing to me but they were on my list. From there, the system fell apart: I couldn't find anyone to help me; the staff were clustered in small groups talking to each other and they treated me like an idiot when I asked questions; they then gave me the wrong items and kept me waiting for over an hour before my problems were solved; they got the bill wrong; and they threw my items into the back of my car.

Basically, they took my money and kicked me out. Typically this business was being directed by a very old adage, one I have covered in this section: the first 30 seconds are vitally important for the customer to form positive opinions about the business.
But this is a waste of time if the entire system falls apart after the first 30 seconds.

There is another adage they should have taken note of; it can take minutes to years to build a great reputation and only minutes to destroy it.

Every single business is set up to sell something to someone. If your customer service can be its very best at every level of the business, you will have to fight customers off with a stick (not a good customer service technique I might add).

Think much bigger than just the front counter/greeter/website/phone call.

For a lot of business owners and managers, this is a daunting task. My advice here is to break your business into components and address each one from a customer service perspective. Over time each component will be dealt with and each improvement will lift your overall level of customer service.

What can you do today?

Look at your own business and consider what steps you are taking to ensure you stay at the front of the pack. Make a list of things you do, 'because that's the way we always do it'.
Ask yourself, honestly, whether there is a better way to do it - trust me there generally is.
Let go of the old and welcome in the new and your business will appreciate it.

Break your business into components or modules so you can assess and review your level of customer service for each individual part. Then start working your way through the list, coming up with ways to improve the customer service offered in each component. If you are stuck for ideas, get your staff involved (a good idea anyway) and get your customers involved (an even better idea).

Who is your biggest competitor?

I've put this section in as almost a word of warning. It's based on a realisation I had when listening to an audiobook. It certainly made me change my mind when it came to who businesses are really up against.

It should certainly focus your mind on why the customer should be respected and they are the kings of your business.

Remember earlier in the book, when I talked about how TESCO became a retailing giant with a particular focus on one thing? The customer?

Fast forward to April 2015, and TESCO announces its worst losses in history and in UK corporate history, (£6.4 billion) and there had become an air of panic around the company. There was a time where, the urban myth would have you believe, that for every £5 spent, £1 of it went to TESCO. But after several investigations, management changes and possible legal challenges to their accounting practices, not only was it perceived as losing market share, it was now perceived as haemorrhaging cash.

One analyst said, *"This was the version of 'kitchen sinking' all their problems in one announcement. In fact, they added the washing machine, the dishwasher, the deep fat fryer...."* (BBC Business Editor Kamal Ahmed).

It was a worry for most people with pensions, a worry for the shareholders and a worry for the colleagues that work in the 3000 UK stores.

People kept bandying the phrase that "discounters were destroying their businesses". Were they the real problem? Yes, to a point they were. However, all of the big 4 supermarkets were also under price pressure from those same discounters and whilst they have lost market share, they too were missing the point as to who their competitor really is. None of them has gone out of business. Aldi and Lidl haven't gone to the top of the tree yet. They haven't become the biggest two in the country yet.

The thing that Terry Leahy got right in his first few years was to "listen" to his competitors. In fact in a lot of industries such as services, (they are selling time and an intangible service, not a product), Harry Beckwith, in his book, "Selling the Invisible", agrees and states that their competitors are not who they think they are.

Who are they?

They are the customer, the prospect and the lead.

Why?

Well, think about it. In retail, they have two choices. Use and buy what you're offering or don't use or buy what you're offering and go somewhere else.

In the service industry, such as choosing a driving instructor they have three! Use and buy your service. Don't do it at all with you. Do it themselves.

Every potential customer has a choice. What Terry Leahy got right is that he understood that. In one of his first moves as the top man at TESCO, he held focus groups with REAL customers and simply asked: "What do you want?" When was the last time you asked any of your customers or prospects that?

All the planning and 'SWOT'ing in the world will never really negate the actual needs of the person that wants to buy the product or service. You can even fill a room full of intelligent people and get them to put a plan for your business together, but it doesn't mean they are going to get it right. Far from it. Eight intelligent TV executives were put in a room once and came up with a sitcom called 'At Home with the Hitler's', (seriously...look for it on YouTube. And this was in the 90's!).

Every customer or prospect, has their own needs, their own barriers, their own wants and depending on how flexible you are, how much you can offer that prospect. By allowing them to feel like they 'own' their own product or service, they are more likely to buy from you, simply because you listened. Then you should price accordingly.

If you don't believe me...

The buzz phrase coming out of what was the UK's biggest and brightest company, which just threw out the kitchen sink. "We need to understand what our customers want...."

It's nice to see they haven't forgotten what Sir Terry did. It's a pity everyone forgets that until it's too late and the kitchen is empty!

CHAPTER 6
MAKE YOUR BUSINESS UNBELIEVABLE!

This is an interesting section, one that really addresses, I believe, the differences between mediocre and winning businesses. The place where you conduct your business should be impressive in a lot of different ways.

Even if you don't have customers visiting your business, surely it is important for your staff to enjoy coming to work and, hopefully, even love coming to work?

The real aim of this section is to identify ways to make your business more appealing to your customers. It even covers how to make YOU and your colleagues impressive too. I haven't seen a business book talk about what to wear before, so we thought we'd get someone to do it for us. The section covers a range of key issues to achieve this goal and, as a result, your business will stand out as a winning business:

- Have pride in your workplace (even if you are the only one there)
- Make your workplace inviting and easy for your customers to visit
- Don't scrimp on the little things (out with *Women's Weekly* 1972 or FHM or Countryside Walking Magazine)
- Offer really good coffee and tea (and nice cups)

- Just add laughter (in vast amounts and often)
- Encourage people to bring their personality to work
- Beware of bad smells
- Who is in control of the music?
- Cleanliness is a key component to profitability
- Make one person the keeper of the workplace

Have pride in your workplace (even if you are the only one there)

When was the last time you walked into a business and went, 'Wow'?

My guess would be not recently, but I hope I'm wrong. Your workplace should be impressive, even if you are the only person working there.

Having pride in your workplace, whether it's static or mobile, means it looks clean and tidy, it is organised and it is ready for business. Too many businesses look run down and worn out - often reflecting the feelings of the business owners. The place might look dirty and grubby, the pictures are crooked, the brochures are in messy piles, none of the furniture matches, there is a very strange smell, the carpet is faded, AC/DC are blaring on a cheap stereo and there is no real sign of life - certainly no feeling of energy or enthusiasm from the staff.

Compare this to the concept of walking into a well-lit, freshly painted business, where all the displays are neat and tidy, the staff are wearing clean, ironed uniforms, there are fresh flowers on the counter and a clean smell throughout, everything looks in place and there is gentle background music playing. That's much more inviting and memorable.

An idea I try to promote throughout this book is the concept of becoming a better observer of other businesses. This is a characteristic that I have seen as a common thread in many very successful entrepreneurs - they look at everything. Whenever you go into a business take a moment to look around - what do they do right and what do they do wrong? And from there, what could you do better?

I think too many workplaces look shocking, specifically in some industries. And I think you know which ones I mean.

They look functional, definitely uninspired and, generally, no one wants to stay there too long. Personally I couldn't imagine working in a place like that. To me, we all spend more time at work than just about anywhere else. I think it is essential my office looks clean, inviting, motivational and welcoming for my customers, my associates and my team.

It's like the business where the front reception is very impressive but as soon as you walk out back it looks like a bomb has gone off. Have pride in your workplace and it will be reflected in everyone who deals with you. Just getting the compliments from your customers is very rewarding, but the overall financial benefits of having a business that looks like you care about it will be even more rewarding because the customers will want to keep coming back.

What can you do today?

Do you really have pride in your workplace?
If you do, congratulations, but now focus on becoming an observer of other businesses to look for ways to make it even better.

If your workplace needs an extreme makeover, today is the day to start planning it. Someone needs to take control of the makeover and if you can't do it, find someone who can.

Make your workplace inviting and easy for your customers to visit.

If you run a business where the customers come to you, make it inviting and easy for them to not only find the business but also to actually get into the business. While it is important to make the business inviting once the customers are inside, if they can't find it or if it doesn't look appealing enough on the outside to go in, the rest can be a waste of time. To make your business easy for your customers to visit there are a number of issues to consider.

Some businesses are so hard to find that for many time-deprived customers they will simply give up and go elsewhere. Good signage to direct people is certainly essential, and if you tend to use directions quoting a street name with a door or unit number it is a wise idea to have that number well signed, (in big print, preferably) in a very visible place.

Making it easy for your customer to park is another good tip. I recently visited a large shopping centre that had reconfigured its car park to try and fit more cars in. Unfortunately they had made all of the parking bays much smaller so it was now a tight squeeze to park and it was also very likely your car would get damaged by people opening doors or moving trolleys around the parked cars. Not a good move. And I'm pleased to say they did change it after listening to their customer's feedback. Easier to have 3 or 4 less car parking spaces, and spend less time on dealing with customer complaints.

The entrance to your business should also be very clearly marked. It can be frustrating to have to wander around the outside of a business trying to figure out how to get inside.

Having a sign of your trading hours in a clearly visible spot also makes it easy for customers to know when the business is open.
To make the entrance inviting it should not be overly cluttered. Creating barriers for people to negotiate can make the business less appealing. This doesn't mean you can't have some products on display outside the business but make sure the access is not blocked.

The front of the business should always be clean and tidy. This should be one of the first jobs done when preparing the business to open up for the day and it should be repeated during the day on a regular basis. I am often surprised at how dirty the fronts of many businesses are. It doesn't make a good impression and, as discussed elsewhere in this book, first impressions are very important.

Having good lighting is another important issue, especially if your customers visit your business at night. We are all a little more aware and concerned about our personal safety these days and a well-lit building is far more appealing than one that isn't.

Every business is different, but the principles are the same. Make your business inviting and appealing and your customers will be more likely to come back. It isn't difficult, but like most of the recommendations in this book it needs someone to put a system in place to make sure it is done.

What can you do today?

How easy is it to find your business?

How appealing is the entrance?

Take a few minutes to walk around it and make a list of things that could be done right now to make it more approachable. Either do those things yourself or put a system in place to make sure they are done on a regular basis throughout the day. If your customers are telling you your business is hard to find, figure out where you can place directional signage and get it happening today.

Don't scrimp on the little things (out with *Women's Weekly* 1972 and FHM and Countryside Walks Magazine)

Every week one of my old bosses spent £50 on flowers for reception. He purchased these from the local markets and they always looked sensational. (We always thought it was a little odd as the place of work was a Supermarket and he could have got them from the shop floor.) We'd get more comments and compliments regarding these flowers than any other part of the business. (That should have told us something I guess.) People visiting would stick their heads in just to tell us how much they liked the flowers.

We have all experienced a visit to a business where the waiting room is filled with ten-year-old magazines that are tattered and torn, or blank walls, or a tired and dusty plastic plant on the counter. These may seem like little things in the scheme of a business but the little things can make all the difference. You really notice this when you visit a business that pays good attention to detail. It is far more inviting and enjoyable to visit. We tend to expect a business to have old magazines but when they are the latest edition we are pleasantly surprised and it makes an impression.

Whatever your business, if people come to you, paying attention to the details that make it more enjoyable for your customers to visit will impress them. They will tell their friends, even if they are not sure why they like the business. Of course, you need to be able to back up the attention to detail with good products and services, but at least your customers are in the right frame of mind when they visit.

What can you do today?

Make a list of five things that you could do better to make your business more appealing to your customers. This process needs to be repeated on a regular basis and, most importantly, the list is only the start.
Actioning the list is the difference between a winning business and a mediocre one.

Offer really good coffee and tea (and nice cups)

If you run a business where your customers tend to spend a little time, you naturally offer them tea and coffee. It really makes a difference if you offer them good coffee and tea and you serve them in nice, clean cups. It reinforces your attention to detail and the value you place on their custom.

Some businesses just fall apart when it comes to this area of service. There isn't any milk, they are out of coffee or, even worse, it is the cheapest coffee available, purchased in giant tins that have been around for ten years, or the cups are dirty and lipstick stained.
If you are going to make the offer, be prepared for your customers to say yes.
Have good quality coffee, fresh milk, a range of teas - remembering that a lot of people drink herbal teas these

days- sugar and sugar substitutes, clean quality cups and a presentable tray to carry it all on.

I am sure that some readers may be thinking, 'Is this really that big a deal?' and my answer is, 'Yes'.
Successful businesses are different from their competitors - and the differences are normally the little things. You're reading a book by a guy who got excited when his local cinema was allowed to serve alcohol. There are only so many first nights of superhero blockbusters you can sit through on a Friday night with teenage kids and nerds without the need for a relaxant.

Being committed to making your business better than your competitors' means, putting that extra effort and energy into looking after your customers.

For those businesses that already do this they know that it works. For those who are unsure, try it and see the response from your customers.

Another good idea includes having good drinking water and clean glasses, or a ready supply of plastic cups.

Having a box of tissues in the office, boardroom and at reception is another simple point that doesn't appear to be a big deal but is another reinforcement of the fact that you care about your customers. (And the people you've just had to let go...joke!)

Magnificent businesses care for their customers and they are prepared to show it.

What can you do today?

How can you show your customers that you care?

You might already serve really good tea and coffee, but there is bound to be another aspect missing that will in some way show you care. Work out what that one thing is and implement it today.

Just add laughter (in vast amounts and often)

I am a very big advocate of having a lot of fun in your workplace. This is a point which I discussed earlier in this book. Having fun is not unprofessional - everyone benefits and people like to be involved.
The most noticeable example I have seen of this in recent times was by a national fresh juice business that has grown to have hundreds of outlets in a very short time. A visit to one of these stores is like visiting the theatre.

The team have a lot of interaction with each other and they laugh, they have fun, they clown around and they generally seem to be having a pretty good time. As a customer it is very refreshing to watch a group of young, energetic people having fun doing what they are doing. It makes the whole experience far more enjoyable. Judging by the way this business is growing, there is no shortage of customers who share my views.

An excellent book that promotes the concept of bringing some fun into the workplace is *Fish* by Stephen Lundin. The author bases his recommendations on his observations of a very successful fish mongering business at the Pike Place Fish Markets in Seattle.
The book has sold millions of copies worldwide so there appears to be a lot of support for the idea that it is not only okay to bring some fun into your workplace, it is actually a very significant method to help build a successful business. Lighten up your business and encourage your team to bring some humour and fun into the workplace. Personally

I believe it will show the colleagues have a degree of confidence in the business when they feel comfortable enough to enjoy themselves.

What can you do today?

If you haven't already purchased a copy of the book 'Fish', today is the day.
Buy it, read it and put some of the author's recommendations into action.
If you have already got a copy sitting on your bookshelf, open it up and pick out a few simple tips and action them.

Encourage people to bring their personality to work

I believe that the days of the faceless employee are over and I say good riddance. Sterile workplaces, nameless faces and an overall sense of being just a number in the machine needed to go. People like personalities and I believe it is something that should be encouraged.

Sure, there is a limit - we can't have people being too over-the-top or gregarious to the point that it is intimidating, but encourage your staff to make work a reflection of themselves- it has many benefits. Most importantly your staff will enjoy their work a lot more. They will tend to be more relaxed and happier and they will feel a sense of ownership regarding the business. If they are enjoying themselves they will offer better levels of service and your customers will notice the difference.

How you encourage people to bring their personality to work is up to you.

It might be personal items at their desk; it might be what they wear or what they say. Bringing personality into a business environment is being encouraged at senior management levels, in fact it is essential, so why not adopt the same principles at all levels of your business.

As a business owner and entrepreneur you bring your own personality and flair to work. Encourage others to do the same and your business will benefit from it.

Here I want to quickly write about a friend of mine that genuinely, not only brings their personality to work, but also their business is an extension of their personality.

Andy Pearson, Rockstar, Business Owner and thoroughly nice chap,

I'd like to introduce you to Andy Pearson, owner of 'Drive Like A Rockstar' Driving School. His business and he personally are so far removed from what a driving school or a driving instructor should be like, it's brilliant and unique.

Andy worked for a major national franchise when he first started. Previous to that he had mainly worked on building sites and within in the construction and electrical industry, so he had almost zero knowledge of an industry that was so cluttered with the 'same old, same old'. He quickly realised that he was not going to make a lot of money working for them. So he sought a fresh perspective on a driving school.

Andy is heavily tattooed. Andy loves rock music. Add those two together and you would think that the answer is the total opposite of what a driving school should be. But, like many people and businesses, people are prone to incorrect misconceptions.

Andy is a thoroughly nice bloke. He's also incredibly skilful at what he does with a fantastic record and a top grading within the industry. He also thought that there was a misconception about some of the students that get into instructors cars when they have tattoo's and love 'Guns and Roses'. His only previous experience of running a business was running a Rock band and because he was proud of his achievements in that industry, targeted an 'audience' rather than customers.

So Andy brought his personality to his business and set up 'Drive Like A Rockstar' and is now expanding. The flamed looking car graphics and even the way he dresses is absolutely 'Rockstar' status. He's also in the regular running for National Awards within the industry. He's recently been filming documentaries, appeared in newspapers, local BBC radio and is a business mentor at his local University. So whilst some may mock, his business has gone from strength to strength, using his personality and his uniqueness as his strength. He attracts the customers that want a unique experience and want to learn with someone that understands and 'gets' what they like in life.

What can you do today?

What is your philosophy towards your staff bringing their personalities to work? Is it something you have actually thought about? Why not sit down with your team and ask them their thoughts. Setting parameters can be a good idea, but as with any boundaries explain to your staff why they are in place.

Beware of bad smells

Funnily enough some businesses really do stink - literally.

A strange thought in the modern world. We live in a world where shops offer about a million chemicals that can mask, destroy, enhance or modify just about any odour known to mankind. But it can be a problem.

In recent years there has been a lot of research done on how human senses affect buying patterns and decisions. Now we know that the visual side of a business is very important, but so are sounds and smells. Anyone walking past a hot chicken shop or a bakery knows the intoxicating effect these odours can have on the casual passerby, often leading them into the shop before they even know they are doing it.

Modern day supermarkets have invested millions of pounds into air-conditioning systems that pump the beautiful smells of freshly baked bread from the back of the store, where the bread is usually kept, to the front.

This theory filters over into other areas of business. Estate agents encourage you to freshly bake things or have freshly made coffee on the go if there is a viewing.

If you work in the same place day in day out, you can start to become oblivious to bad odours. I believe one particular brand of air freshener calls it 'nose blind'. To you they are normal smells rather than offensive smells, but to your customers they may be a significant turn off.

Again the human mind takes over and assimilates all of the information it receives. A dodgy smell creates the assumption that the business may be dodgy.

Equally as bad are those businesses where someone has discovered an oil burner and they are determined to stew lavender oil every minute of every day.

Sure the smell may be nice occasionally, and in small doses, but it is very strong and overpowering.

The very worst scenario is a food-based business that smells bad. Bad smells and food do not go well together in the same sentence, let alone in the same breath. Be aware of any bad or overpowering smells - they could be costing you business. Neutrality is the best path.

What can you do today?

Does your business stink? Hopefully not, but it might be worth doing the smell test and then addressing the issue to prevent possible loss of customers due to offensive or overpowering smells.

Who is in control of the music?

Loud or inappropriate music in a business can turn customers away in droves.
It is often a point overlooked or not given a lot of attention. Like all of the tips in this section, the aim is to make your business as appealing as possible to your customers. If the music is wrong or too loud, it isn't going to make your customers come in or stay and you will lose out.
I actively encouraged people to bring their personality to work but I am not sure this is appropriate when it comes to music - sorry.

Have you ever sat in a restaurant with a friend and found it is impossible to carry on a conversation because the music is too loud?
Have you ever walked into a shop only to leave a few minutes later because you're not into the latest Megadeath hit?

Sure we all have our own musical tastes and one person's Beethoven is another person's Sex Pistols, but the important point here is to figure out what is appropriate for your customers, not your team. (Although I did find the entrance of a Bride-to-Be to Iron Maiden's 'Bring Your Daughter to the Slaughter' at a wedding I attended incredibly funny.)

Just like smells, sounds have a lot of associated psychology. Research shows that some music does have an impact on a shopper's buying habits. In restaurants the faster the beat of the music the faster people tend to eat. So if you run a restaurant that focuses on high turnover with diners not spending a lot of time in the restaurant, music with a fast beat is appropriate. If you are running a fine dining establishment where patrons have the table for the night, it is preferable they take their time and hopefully purchase more food and beverages in doing so.

The same applies for music over the telephone system .The only thing worse than being on hold for five minutes with no music is being on hold for ten minutes with deafening music that forces you to hold the hand piece at arm's length.

The message here is to be aware of music and the role it plays in your business. Make it appropriate for your particular customers and make one person responsible for the music. This person needs to be given the appropriate guidelines for what to play and how loud it should be. They then make sure it happens.

What can you do today?

Think about the role music plays in your business.
If you can incorporate it that is great, but assign one person to be in charge of the music according to some very clear guidelines.

Then let the rest of your team know and understand the importance of music and what is appropriate and what is not.

Cleanliness is a key component to profitability

Earlier I spoke about the power of smells to have an impact on your business. Well, cleanliness can be a related issue but generally it deserves its own attention.

I am amazed at the number of businesses that are downright filthy. A few years back, I had to purchase a set of tyres for my car and I had to wait while they were being fitted. Let me describe the waiting room.

There were two couches, covered in grime and grit where the workers sat during their breaks. There was a coffee table filled with really old, ragged magazines, all revealing various forms of semi-naked ladies promoting things to do with cars. There was a collection of cracked and broken cups baked in residue that had to be pre-World War I. There was coffee and sugar everywhere and a television playing Radio 2. To top it off, there was an overflowing ashtray that probably hadn't been emptied since people stopped smoking indoors. Now I was the first customer in this business on that day and I was greeted with this sight. If I knew I had to wait in a tip I wouldn't have gone there and I certainly didn't go back. I see no excuse for this kind of mess, which is wrong in so many ways that I could write a book about it.

I stopped visiting a local coffee shop simply because it was always filthy. The tables were always covered in used cups and plates and as its seating was outdoors, the wind blew everything around. Added to this was the local pigeon population, which had figured out that this was an excellent foraging ground for left over morsels. So in amongst the refuse was the added delight of pigeon droppings. All in all, it's not a very attractive place to stop for a coffee and piece of cake.

To top it off, there was often four or five staff standing behind the counter waiting for a customer to turn up rather than going outside to clean up the mess. This was clearly just a poorly run business and one that has since cleaned up its act, I must say, but I am still emotionally scarred and hesitant to go there.

I certainly would not order food from this business - if they could let the front of the business get so filthy what is the kitchen like?

Many retail shops and even offices are really dirty and grubby and there is no excuse for that. Customers expect, and I believe they are entitled, to visit a clean business. One area where a lot of businesses really lose customers is their toilets.
Sure, keeping public toilets clean can be tough, but filthy toilets are a very big turn off for many consumers - they will go to a business where they know the toilets are clean, even if the products or services being sold are not as good. What's really annoying are the toilets in bars and pubs that are meant to have staff signing to say they've checked them for levels of cleanliness?

To those pubs and bars, I say, please don't think we don't know that bit of paper is a 'paper filling exercise' to get health and safety off your back should someone fall down and bang their heads on the U-bend. Should any local authority Health and Safety go into Pubs and Bars in a work capacity on a Friday or Saturday night, they'll soon see the paper on the toilet door is just that...a bit of paper.

Actually I'm being a little unfair on pubs and bars trying to keep their toilets clean on a Friday and Saturday night when the place is heaving...it would be a pointless and thankless task, but I'm trying to make a point here.

A business that is not clean shows a lack of respect for itself, its customers and its staff. A winning business rarely has this problem.

What can you do today?

How clean is your business?
Have a walk around and make a list of ten things you could do today to make your business cleaner and more appealing to everyone who deals with you.

Make one person the keeper of the workplace

Often the hardest part about making your workplace truly winning is that there is no one person charged with this responsibility. I strongly recommend you make one person the 'keeper of the workplace' and their responsibility is to make sure the business always looks sounds and smells its best.

If you are going to give this person that kind of responsibility (and for those single-person businesses I guess it's up to you) they will need to know exactly what is expected of them and most importantly why it is expected.

Often these kinds of expectations can be seen as the semi-neurotic ramblings of an unreasonable business owner rather than the significant business essentials that they are.

I believe the person in charge of keeping the workplace perfect plays one of the most essential roles within an organisation and it is important they are made aware of it. Even though one person is committed to being in charge, everyone needs to work together to keep the business in the right outward shape. This is a trap that can easily snare the unwary. The other members of the team start to think it's not their responsibility so they stop washing cups or cleaning up after them.
They can walk past rubbish on the floor and dismiss bad smells as someone else's problem, not theirs. So the

keeper of the workplace will still need some support from the powers that be to make sure they aren't left to carry the entire workload.

What can you do today?

Assign your own keeper of the workplace and make sure you let everyone else know they have to pull their weight as well.

CHAPTER 7
MARKETING ON A TIGHT BUDGET

Very few businesses have unlimited funds when it comes to marketing and, naturally, the opposite is more the case: the business needs to do a lot of marketing on a tight budget. This is not a problem but the key to success when it comes to low-cost marketing is that it will involve effort rather than expenditure. Any expenditure you do make, needs to get a return on investment, (R.O.I.). Whilst we are looking at low cost marketing, please don't start believing they spend a £1 and reach 60,000 people on social media. Yes, you can do that, but unless your product, shop or service has a mass appeal, then you are probably reaching the wrong 60,000 people.

This section looks at the key principles behind low-cost marketing and it makes some suggestions on how you can apply this principle to virtually any business.

Things we will cover in this section:

- You have to stand out from the crowd
- If your budget is small you need to put in some elbow grease
- Ask people to send you business and they will
- Networking is not a dirty word
- Learn to introduce yourself and your business
- Always be prepared for an opportunity

- Give away products or services to promote your business
- You need to commit time to marketing
- The Internet is here to stay—and it is amazing
- The power of the testimonial
- Do less but do it well

You have to stand out from the crowd

Before you can even think about marketing your business you need to be committed to making your business stand out from the crowd. But what does this really mean?

It means that every part of your business has to be better than your competitors. The way the business looks, the service you offer, the products or services you sell, your staff, your corporate image—the lot.

I have spoken about the threat of ever-increasing competition and how it impacts all businesses around the world. It is here to stay and it will keep increasing. For a business to truly succeed it needs to be better than its competitors in every way and this requires commitment and dedication from everyone involved in the business. All of the recommendations put forward in this book highlight how to stand out from the crowd in a host of areas but unless that commitment is in place, nothing else will really get off the ground.

A lot of businesses set out with the goal of being average and they achieve it perfectly. But the real gems, the winning ones, know they want to be better than everyone else and they set out with this goal very clearly established. What if your business has been operating for a while—and you are finding yourself being swamped by competitors that are bigger and bolder?

Personally, I really don't think it matters and I certainly don't think that size has a lot to do with it.

You can change your business philosophy today and start making the changes that are required to really make your business stand out from the crowd.

One of the other main reasons you need to drive the 'stand out from the crowd' philosophy is the price. If you offer the same product, the same service and the same benefits, then the ONLY way potential customers or clients can see a difference when making a choice is price. This is where you start getting into the area of price cutting, which is the last place you want to be. Remember you are in business to make money and not lose it.

What can you do today?

Make the commitment right now that you want your business to be the very best it can be. Accept nothing less and you will achieve your goal.

If your budget is small you need to put in some elbow grease

I often spoken to business owners who have the perception that building a successful business requires a lot of money. From my own experiences and observations this is not necessarily true. There are countless examples of businesses that have had big cash injections to get started and they failed, miserably.

Likewise there are countless examples of businesses that started on a shoestring and ended up as huge corporations. (Think Apple and Microsoft)

Money can help but it is by no means the be-all and end-all when it comes to building a successful business, and this is particularly relevant when you talk marketing.
The simple reality is that if you haven't got a big budget to spend on marketing your business, you need to be prepared to roll up your sleeves and do some hard work yourself. It's easy to spend a lot of money on advertising.

Full-page ads in newspapers, on television and radio and most other forms of high-profile advertising will certainly get the phone ringing or the customers coming in the door, but it costs a lot of money. Often the return is nowhere near what you expect.

Low-cost marketing means you have to look for ways to market and promote yourself that generally require effort rather than budget.

I know a business owner who does makeovers on balconies and courtyards and any other small spaces. She had a limited budget but enough money to have some nice brochures printed, which explained exactly what she did. My advice to her was to hit the pavements and put her brochures in the letterbox of every house, apartment that looked like it could do with a makeover in town and to her credit that is exactly what she did. Today she has built a very successful business from being prepared to put in that elbow grease.

There are literally too many examples of ways to market a business for very little money. The best piece of advice I can give is to buy a book that specialises on this topic. 'Guerrilla Marketing' by Jay Conrad Levinson is full of ideas and recommendations that fit into this category. There are also lots of others and they all generally contain great recommendations and tips that will cost very little money.

The aim of this tip is to get you thinking about low-cost marketing ideas and accept the fact that to make them 'happen' the biggest requirement will be someone's time and effort.

What can you do today?

Pop down to your local bookstore and buy a book on low-cost marketing ideas. If you are not sure which one to buy talk to other people in your network and you will find someone who will make a good recommendation. Buying the book is only the start, though. Putting the recommendations into place is the real key—commit to implementing one idea every day.

Ask people to send you business and they will

Often one of the greatest sources of new business comes from referrals. Winning businesses tend to get more than their fair share of referrals from happy customers and this is a pretty good indication that what they are doing, they are doing well.

Surprisingly though, many of us often forget to ask our customers to refer business to us. Sometimes they need to be reminded.

If you have happy customers (and I certainly hope you do), take a few minutes to ask them to tell their family, friends and workmates about you. Often people simply overlook referring business because they don't think to do it. But if you ask them to do it they will go out of their way.

The end result can often be that you build this wonderful network of people, all spreading the word about how wonderful your business is. Now imagine how much your business will grow if every customer you have today recommends you to just one other person. Potentially your business could double overnight.

How do you ask your customers to refer your business? There are a couple of options and it really depends on the type of business you run. A consulting firm might simply make it a closing statement at the end of the project: 'Thank you for your business and please tell your associates about the work we do'. It may be more formal, by mail, or a sign on the wall that says, 'If you are happy with what we do please tell your friends'. Unfortunately most of us are a little hesitant to ask for business and it really is something that needs to be overcome.

I recently gave advice to a clothing retailer about asking for referrals from their existing customers. I suggested they take the approach of talking to their customers and saying that they are looking to grow the business by attracting more customers.

This meant their buying power would be greater so their existing customers would get even better value for money as prices might drop. This strategy worked well because not only did the existing customers take on the sales responsibility, they also had an incentive to promote the business. Everyone wins.

Winning businesses are built on word of mouth and it costs nothing. But you only get it if you deserve it.

What can you do today?

Think of a way to provide an incentive to get your customers to refer business to you and then get them working as your unpaid sales team.

Networking is not a dirty word

Networking is a 'buzz word', (and I do hate 'buzz words'), we all hear all of the time. Unfortunately for many business owners it evokes powerful images of standing around a room with a lot of people you don't know, feeling awkward and unsure. Networking is really just an excellent way to build a business. It's cheap, it's instant and it doesn't require a lot of exceptional skills.

Networking is about communication. Feeling awkward when meeting new people can be challenging but there are many simple techniques to make it easier. I learned a lot of my communication skills from a book I read at least once a year, 'How to win friends and influence people' by Dale Carnegie. The title sounds terribly manipulative but it really isn't.

It is a book about communicating and the lessons learnt from those pages can be used time and time again, every day of the week. The end result will be that you will become a better communicator and you will find networking much easier.

The next part of the process is to go to a networking function with a clear goal. Your aim here is to meet people who might be potential customers or who might be able to refer business to you. Consider a few things ahead of time. Think about how you will introduce yourself and what you sell. If you meet someone who could become a customer or business associate how will you arrange to follow up? How will you end the conversation so that you can move on and meet other people without offending the person you are talking to?

I know some entrepreneurial types who sit down and write a networking plan before they go to these functions, and they get excellent results. It is a business opportunity, not a social event, and they treat it as such.

Networking is here to stay. The better you are at it the more business you can attract. Go into any networking situation with an open mind and with a plan of attack.

What can you do today?

There are two things: the first is to buy a copy of How to win friends and influence people. It will give you some excellent ideas on dealing with people and if you apply them your networking will become much easier. The next thing you can do right now is plan your next networking opportunity. Think about how you will introduce yourself, (see the next section), what questions you will ask the people you meet, (see the short section on FORM on page 58), and how you will excuse yourself when it is time to move on and meet someone else. By simply being prepared you will find that networking can change from a chore to an enjoyable and rewarding experience

Learn to introduce yourself and your business

There are a few different ways to introduce yourself and here I'll cover a few. Remember, first impressions last. If you're not slick, confident and comfortable with what you say, people will remember you as the person that is not slick, confident or comfortable and may not think of you at all when it comes to doing business with you.

The Elevator Pitch- This comes from an introduction that needs to be made in a quick, unexpected way. Imagine you are about to get into a lift, (or elevator if you're outside the

UK), and as the doors shut Bill Gates, Steve Jobs, Sir Richard Branson, (Please feel free to change a name here), steps in with you. You are both going to the top floor. It takes thirty seconds to get to the top. They turn to you and ask, "So...what do you do?"

You've got thirty seconds to come up with something that will spark their interest in you and lead to conversation.

But what can you convey to them that will make you stand out or at least spark their interest?

As a business we all service a need. The 'need' differs from business to business, but there must be a 'need' for any customer to buy your product or service.

I'm going to use a driving school as an example. One of the main reasons being that anybody you introduce yourself to will assume that you and your business all do the same things. The same could be said about solicitors, accountants, human resources, business coaches, garage owners, florists, web designers, photographers. Actually any business we don't use or understand properly.

So the easiest elevator pitch in the driving instructor industry is, *"You know how teenagers want to learn to drive? I fix that."* Simple and to the point. But not quite enough.

Now put your speciality within that sentence.

I'll use an educational issue with in this one, so it now becomes, *"You know how teenagers with Dyspraxia can have issues with co-ordination when they learn to drive? I fix that."*

This has a double 'win'. If the person you are talking to doesn't know there can be issues for pupils with Dyspraxia, then they will ask more. If the person does know there maybe some issues, they will ask you how you fix it.

Simple and to the point, but will generate interest and conversation in those awkward elevator moments.

The One Minute Intro - I was introduced to this by Robert Craven, author of business books such as 'Bright Marketing' and 'Kick Start Your Business', Director, thought leader and a thoroughly nice chap.

The one minute formula, in my eyes is a bit more of an extension of the 'elevator pitch' in that you disclose a little more of what you do and how you do it. The idea behind this is so that you can engage in the art of conversation, in a world where social media rules, the art of conversation is dying.

The process behind the 'One Minute Formula' encourages conversation and may be very important should you find yourself a) in a room full of other businesses that are the same as yours and b) at a networking event where somebody may well be interested in hiring your services.

Now in this introduction, I would also like you to consider adding something else into the mix. According to Simon Sirnek, (YouTube: Search: Simon Sirnek TED Golden Circle), you need to display the reason WHY you do this job.

WHY you offer your service. WHY you do what you do.

When you watch the video, Simon refers to APPLE as a shining light as to WHY they became No.1 in their field. Remember there were 100's of mp3 players on the market before the iPods arrived on the scene. So WHY did we buy from them and not carry on with what we had, which at that point in the time was similar?

He also refers to Wright brothers, those of first to fly fame. He shows you WHY they were successful and the more likely to succeed versus the millions of dollars of the US Government, who were also trying to make a manned flight.

I also highly recommend his book "Start With Why". Thought provoking and gets people thinking about inspiring others to buy or follow you.

So in your introduction you need to get this across as quickly as possible and if you do it right, it's easy to convert to your website and tell visitors WHY they should BUY products or services from you.

Oh...and by the way. It should also pass the 13 year old test. But have you ever tried to get a 13 year old to really listen to what an adult is saying? In other words, what you say and write should be understandable by a 13 year old. It's that simple and keeps the attention of a teenager...no mean feat then!

It runs on simple formula:

- "I / We Work With..."
- "Who Have A Problem With..."
- "What We Do Is..."
- "So That..."
- "Which Means That..."

Again, from a continuity point of view, I'll use the example of a driving school again.

We work with –

This includes the type of business and the age of your business as well as the types of people you work with (including sex/colour/creed)

For Example: *"FRESH has been working with pupils that have educational needs for the last 2 years...."*

Who have a problem with –

Focus on what is wrong for them or what hurts.

For example, *"...that have been unable to learn to drive because they haven't found a suitable driving instructor."*

What we do is-

Be clear and simple so that a 13 year old can understand it and describe HOW you do what you do.

For example, *" What we do is we work with the pupils to understand how they learn and then use various techniques geared to them..."*

So that-

Give a simple explanation of the function that the user/client/pupil/instructor will get.

For example, *"...so that they learn in a calm and encouraging environment."*

Which means-

List the benefits of why that is important.

For example, *"Which means these pupils are included into a society where learning to drive and passing your test is just another aspect of growing up."*

So the final example goes together like this-

"FRESH has been working with pupils that have an educational need for the last 2 years that have been unable to learn to drive because they haven't found a suitable

instructor. What we do is work with pupils to understand how they learn and then use various techniques geared to them, so that can learn in calm and encouraging environments. Which means these pupils are included into a society where learning to drive and passing your test is just another aspect of growing up."

There...that's better than "I'm a driving instructor that teaches people to drive and pass their test."

The sentiment is still the same but in that introduction, we've introduced the 'Value' of what we do and 'Why'. If they are interested, they should buy lessons from the driving school.

What can you do today?

The really important key to its success in real life, (and not only on a business plan), is to be able to say it as it 'rolls off your tongue'. There is nothing cool about stumbling all over it as you make it up on the spot.

Think about it in such a way that when you do say it or write it, no-one can come back and say "So what?"

Always be prepared for an opportunity

The potential for a new customer is always just around the corner and the astute business owner and entrepreneur knows this fact well. They are always ready for action.

To truly take advantage of any opportunity you need to be prepared. You need to keep a supply of business cards on you and your promotional material handy and be ready to talk to someone about what you do.
A common theme promoted in this book is that many business owners are outwardly shy when it comes to

talking about their business. They are almost afraid of saying what they do. STOP IT! While the humility is nice, it really isn't a good strategy for building a business.

Look for any opportunity to promote your business and you will find plenty of them. Look at any chance encounter as an opportunity—who knows what will come out of it? I have made a surprising number of excellent contacts and customers from people I have sat next to on planes, or been forced to wait in queue with, or just bumped into for some reason. If you are generally interested in other people, you will find they will reciprocate and be interested in you.

I am not advocating you stalk people, just that you be prepared to tell people about your business and be prepared to give them more information—never judge a book by its cover. I have come across a lot of people who at first glance may look more like they need a job rather than being in a position to give me work and it is easy to judge based on appearances alone. But by keeping an open mind you will not categorise people as quickly and the potential for a new customer could be standing right in front of you.

Interestingly, the starting point here is being able to say what it is you do. A lot of people actually struggle with this part of the interaction. When asked what they do there is a kind of mumble with downcast eyes. I recommend you have a very clear line in your mind: when asked what you do, stop, look the person in the eye and tell them loudly and proudly.

What can you do today?

Are you prepared for any opportunity?

Do you keep business cards and promotional material readily accessible?
When asked what you do, do you answer in a loud and proud manner or do you mumble and look away?
Today is the day to end bad habits and improve on good ones.

Give away products or services to promote your business

This is the 'put your money where your mouth is principle'. While it might not work for all businesses it will work for most. If what you sell is as good as you say it is, be prepared to give potential customers a free trial or taste. People love FREE!

When was the last time you went into a supermarket and saw something with 50% extra FREE or something like that? Then purchased whatever it is, even though you don't actually need it?

How many times have you signed up to things on social media, because it's a FREE report or a free eBook or a FREE trial of a service or product? We just love FREE!

I recently worked on a marketing campaign with a fitness studio. They wanted to promote personal training as it was a good source of revenue for the business.

At the end of the day we could have advertised special introductory offers to get the people in the doors but it was agreed that the best way to sell the service was to actually give potential customers a free personal training session. Now this was a big expense for the business but they felt their service and the overall personal training they offered was the best available, so they put their money where their mouth was.

It paid off incredibly well. They promoted personal training sessions to their existing members as well as to the general public and they literally doubled their number of personal training clients in a very short amount of time. Of the FREE sessions they gave away in the trial period they retained 85% of the clients and turned them into paying clients.

This no risk, no commitment trial is a good option for customers. They can try a product or business without obligation and it is up to the business to sell itself.
If they don't measure up, the customer can walk away.

I often recommend to my clients to try this technique when looking for ways to build up their business and I have seen it work very successfully in businesses as diverse as restaurants, dance academies, training organisations, bakeries, filtered water suppliers, cleaning product manufacturers and professional service-based businesses. In my own business I offer a one-hour free consultation. This provides potential clients with the opportunity to assess the advice offered by my firm. If they like what they hear they come back, if they don't I never see them again.

Nine out of ten people come back and I put a lot of this high success rate down to the fact that the client has the opportunity to make their own mind up in a non-pressured way with a clear understanding of what my business can offer them.

If you think your business is as good as it can be, try embracing the concept of a free trial or free product and enjoy the results. Analyse what it will cost you to make this offer and monitor the results. You may be pleasantly surprised.

What can you do today?

Can you offer a free product or service as a trial to potential customers?
Why not trial it with a few potential customers and see how it works before you mass market the idea?
You may want to keep this option as a clincher when it comes to closing a deal.

You need to commit time to marketing

I mentioned at the beginning of this section that if you haven't got a lot of money to spend on marketing you need to commit your time to it. One of the biggest reasons for businesses failing to market themselves is that they don't allocate enough time to the process.

Successful businesses are normally good marketers and networkers. They know it is important and they make sure they devote the time necessary to market their business regularly.   This is the key to their success, not the amount they spend.

Marketing needs to become as important as opening the front doors in the morning. It needs the same attention as paying your bills or collecting money from your customers because it determines the long-term success of your business. But because it is less tangible and generally less demanding (if you don't do your marketing no one rings and chases you) it is easy to put off for another day.
Another factor is the average business owner doesn't really know how to market. They are good at what they do but not at marketing, which is logical.

You can learn how to market. You can use your network of business associates and mentors to learn. If you ask people they will normally be very forthcoming in telling you what works for them. There are plenty of good courses that offer simple marketing skills for all levels of business experience, or else you can pay for a marketing consultant to teach you. Regardless of how you improve your skills, the point is you need to commit time to marketing.
In your diary and weekly schedule, there should be blocks of time marked out for when you focus on nothing but marketing your business.

How much time? That's up to you.

The more time you spend marketing the greater the results will tend to be but if you spend all of your time marketing and no time running your business the end result could be lots of new customers who leave because the business is poorly run. Clearly it depends on the size of your business and your support staff.

What can you do today?

Go through your diary and block out time for the next week, and for all the weeks after when you can spend time on marketing your business.
It must be adhered to.

If you are not sure where to start, read a book that tells you how to market. Set up your files so that all of your material is at your fingertips.

Meet with your business associates and mentors to get their advice and recommendations, but start it today.

The Internet is here to stay—and it is amazing

I am a big believer in the power of the Internet. As a marketing tool it is unequalled in many ways. It's cost effective, it's convenient for customers to use, there are plenty of companies that can help you take advantage of it and it is used by more potential customers every day. BUT, and as you can see it is a BIG BUT, be careful...it can suck your money dry also.

The role the Internet plays in our everyday lives just keeps increasing. Ten years ago the thought of being able to pay all of your bills from your computer would have been a dream, now it is as normal as watching television. There is nothing that cannot be purchased over the net and businesses are becoming more and more creative about how to use the Internet to grow their business.

From a marketing point of view the Internet provides a very accessible way for customers to find out more about your business. They can do this at a time that suits them and without the added pressure of facing a salesperson. They can form an opinion of your business in the privacy of their own home, and this is exactly what they do.

Customers will use the net to research businesses. They will use it to find out more about the businesses that can provide whatever product or service they require. If your business is not online and your competitors are, they have a distinct advantage.

Having a good website is the bare minimum for any business. It should be professionally designed, visually impressive and easy to use. Design your website from a customer's perspective: what information would they like to see and how would they need to navigate the site? If you need to have lots of information, then arrange it in a way that doesn't make the site overly complicated or filled with page after page of information. Have easy-to-download information in PDF software so the format of the information doesn't change when it is printed out. Include pictures of you and your business—but make sure the site loads quickly; remember we are all short of time and there is nothing more frustrating than waiting for what seems like an eternity for a website to load.

I still encounter people in 2015, who think the Internet is a waste of time. No matter how much I try to convince them otherwise they have formed their opinion and it is unlikely to change. Generally these people don't use the net a lot themselves or they have a bad website that doesn't really work. They formulate their opinion based on the lack of traffic flow to their site. Having the site is just the start; driving traffic to it is the next part.

 A web development company can advise you on how to increase traffic and this topic is a whole book in its own right.

The fact is, though, it can be done and it isn't necessarily complicated or expensive. BUT and again it's a BIG BUT, I have come across people that try and 'sell you the dream' that you MUST be on page one of Google or other search engines, to be successful.

Successful businesses accept and embrace the Internet as PART of their overall marketing strategy and not ALL of it.

What can you do today?

If you don't have a website, get the wheels in motion to make one happen today. Get a website designed and built to your budget—if you can only afford a one-page site, fine; grow it over time as you can afford it.

If you do have a website talk to your developer about how you can make it better and increase traffic flow on a budget you can manage.

The power of the testimonial

Testimonials are used to build credibility and they need to be a part of any marketing material you produce. Basically they are endorsements of your business from satisfied customers. Large companies use them all the time, most noticeably with high-profile celebrities endorsing their products and services.

There is no reason why small businesses can't use testimonials just as effectively.

Testimonials help potential customers to make up their mind about using a new business because they are going by the recommendation of a third person.
All businesses will tell you how great they are but to have an independent customer sharing their experience is far more convincing.

Collecting testimonials is easy (assuming you have plenty of happy customers). Every business should have a number of customers who are loyal and they are normally more than happy to offer a comment about your business. Asking for a written testimonial is fine; if they haven't got the time to write something down get them to do a verbal testimonial and copy it down.

Make absolutely certain though that the customer is happy for you to use their testimonial in marketing material. It is a little rude to assume that this is okay as some people may take offence if they are not asked. I like to actually get them to sign a release simply stating that the testimonial given is okay to be used.

The types of comments you are after are the ones that will state how satisfied the customer is with your business, products or services. Testimonials are recommendations so they are even more powerful if the customer states how long they have been using the business, why they use it and the fact that they intend to keep using it. This all helps to reinforce the message that your business, product or service is good.

Collecting testimonials can be time consuming and unfortunately most of us wait until we need them before collecting them. This makes the whole process a bit of a rush and often it gets forgotten or is put in the too hard basket.

I recommend you collect testimonials on a regular basis and keep them in a folder. That way, as soon as you need them they are at your fingertips ready to be used. Testimonials can be printed on brochures, listed on your website, hung on the wall of your business or used in your advertising.

What can you do today?

Start collecting testimonials today. Build up a supply that you can use in all of your promotional material.

Do less but do it well

When it comes to marketing there is a lot of value in the statement that it is better to do less but do what you do well. Rather than trying to action fifty great marketing ideas poorly, implement ten exceptionally well. These ten ideas then form a very solid and dependable core to your business' marketing activity.

Further to this, it is much easier to monitor what is working and what is not and this is important when it comes to marketing. After all, what is the point of doing marketing if it doesn't work.

Like any business-related activity the dreaded FTI (failure to implement) is always lurking close by. If your 'to do' list is too long, it is more likely you won't get anything done which, as discussed previously, can have serious ramifications for your business.

The marketing process has more steps in it than most people realise. Each is equally important and it is easy to see that trying to do lots is not going to be as effective as taking a more strategic view to the entire process. The following list is a good guideline to understanding the steps involved in the marketing process from the beginning.

- Do your homework on your potential customers—who exactly do you want to do business with?
- Find out about your competitors—what they are offering—and determine what makes your business different.
- Establish your goals and objectives and be very clear about them.
- Get your product right.
- Develop your corporate image.
- Develop your promotional material.
- Determine how you will market to your targeted customers.

- Start implementing your marketing.
- Monitor and evaluate what you are doing.
- Keep marketing.
- Take a more controlled approach to your marketing—aim to do less but do it well and your business will enjoy greater results.

What can you do today?

What is your philosophy towards marketing? Are you trying to do lots without actually doing what you do well? Address each of the steps in the marketing process and identify which areas you need to improve to add more impact to your marketing.

CHAPTER 8
IF YOU CAN'T SELL HOW CAN YOU SUCCEED?
THE NON-SALES CHAPTER

The whole reason any of us are in business is to sell something. Yet often this seems to be overlooked. Business owners build magnificent looking businesses and promote them extensively but when you finally pick up the phone or go into the business, their selling skills and abilities are terrible. You walk out in disgust.

I am in no way advocating the hard sell or the pressure sell. Good selling skills are simply good customer service. People expect the person answering the phone or standing behind the counter to be able to meet their needs or at least point them in the direction of someone who can. Lousy selling skills are rampant in modern business, generally because of a lack of commitment from business owners to train staff due to the expense. Of course this is crazy, because the better your staff sell the more profitable the business will become.

In this section we will cover:

- Do you really know what you are selling?
- Why should someone buy what you are selling?
- To be good at selling you have to be good at listening
- Get someone in to teach your staff how to sell—regularly

- Do you make it easy for people to buy from you?
- How you sold yesterday may not apply to how you sell today or tomorrow
- Become a sales analyser—every time you put your hand in your pocket
- How do you monitor your sales?
- What is the customer's main concern in the sales process?
- Always ask for the sale

Do you really know what you are selling?

I recently watched a sales training seminar for a group of people in a mobile phone company. When they started to talk about product knowledge it soon became apparent that everyone in the group had different knowledge regarding the various products offered by the business and a lot of the information was conflicting.

They had to stop and address each product and get the facts. A lack of product knowledge is a common problem and it is extremely frustrating for customers.

The reason for this lack of product knowledge and a general lack of sales skills is simply that a lot of people end up in sales rather than follow a set course to get there. One day they find themselves in a sales role and they simply do the best they can.

To make sure everyone involved in selling within your business is up to speed there has to be a very good level of communication. Time has to be spent talking about the products and services offered and this needs to be done regularly. Business runs at a pretty hectic pace these days and there is a mass of information available which often makes it hard to rummage through to find the facts among the hype.

Once you have product knowledge you need to be able to make a recommendation.

This is another step in the sales process where many salespeople struggle. They can't make a recommendation based on what the customer is asking for—all they can do is give the customer options.

Do whatever it takes to make sure your team are as knowledgeable as possible about the products and services you sell and your business will definitely stand out from the competition. If you need help why not get your suppliers to do presentations about the products that you sell.

What can you do today?

What steps can you take to make sure you and your team have the best level of product knowledge for everything you sell in your business?
Implement one activity today that will get the process moving.

Why should someone buy what you are selling?

This is a good question and one that needs to be answered by anyone involved in selling for your business. Why should a customer buy from you?
It is an interesting question and one I always ask when I am running a workshop.

Apart from product knowledge related questions it is often the hardest question to answer. As an exercise, ask anyone in your business that is in a selling role why they think a customer should buy from them. The range of answers will probably be eye-opening.

This question requires an answer developed by all of your staff. Have a meeting and work through it until you can come up with the definitive statement. And it needs to be convincing—big and bold, not 'wishy washy' and lukewarm. Once you have a statement it needs to be introduced into every sales pitch, even if the customer doesn't ask the question. The customer will be thinking it so why not take control of the situation and let them know. It can be introduced by a statement such as, "and you are probably wondering why you should buy this from us, not a competitor—well the answer is ...."

The reason why someone should buy what you are selling may change over time. It is a concept that needs to be revisited on a regular basis and it should be freely discussed. Try different versions of the definitive statement you have created.

Does it close the deal or does the customer walk out when you say it?

If they do, what you are saying is not convincing enough and it is time to go back to the drawing board.

What can you do today?

Have you got your definitive, 'Why should you buy from this business' statement?
If not, today is the day to develop it. Get your staff involved and be prepared to talk about this concept a lot. When it stops working change it.

To be good at selling you have to be good at listening

Ironically many salespeople miss the point when it comes to selling. They feel that to be a good salesperson you have to talk a lot and you need to talk fast.
I think it is safe to say we are all over this kind of approach to selling.

To be truly good at selling you have to be good at two things. Firstly you have to be good at asking questions. But most importantly, you have to be very good at listening to the answers the customer gives. Remember the saying, "God gave you two ears and one mouth. Use them in that proportion."

We have all experienced quality sales service—you get asked intelligent questions and are then informed about your options based on the information you have given. Ideally you are then recommended a particular product or service. Perfect and really not that complicated. The 'normal' sales approach is to maybe ask you a token, parrot-like question ignore your answer and then go into a sales speech based on what the salesperson wants to sell not what you, the customer, want to buy.

Listening is easier said than done. For a lot of people nerves make them talk a lot. Meeting a customer can be intimidating so they compensate by talking too fast and too much. Take a breath and get the customer to do the talking and you will be well and truly on the way to better sales performance.

If your salespeople are not good listeners, your business may be doomed to stay in the realms of mediocrity.

What can you do today?

Think about how you and your staff sell. Be a fly on the wall. Do you make the same mistakes as most salespeople and if you do, try the new approach the next time you serve a customer.

Get someone in to teach your staff how to sell—regularly

If you want your staff to sell more—train them. Give them the necessary skills to be good at selling and they will not only sell more they will also enjoy their job a lot more. Even though selling is not an overly complicated process or set of skills it does have a certain daunting feel to it that can be intimidating for some people. If they know how to overcome these feelings everyone wins.

I knew someone that sold encyclopaedias door-to-door. Now that was a job where if you didn't sell you didn't eat. Your selling skills had to be pretty sharp. He had a supervisor who sat down with the team at the beginning of every shift to go over our sales techniques and skills. It really did get him in the right frame of mind before being unleashed on the suburbs of leafy Worcestershire. (He also sold the 'Pools' and he must have done a really good job. My dad did them for about ten years and I can't remember him winning a penny.)

If your staff need training it is generally better to get in an expert, someone who teaches people to sell all the time. They will be able to iron out problems quickly. With a good sales trainer you should notice an improvement in your figures pretty much straight away.

How often you get the trainer in is up to you. They will normally be able to put a programme together that will get the results you expect. Sales are sales, regardless of the business you are in. The techniques are generally the same so, even if you think your business is different or unique, they can be applied appropriately.

Successful businesses realise that well-trained sales staff are essential to making and keeping the business profitable.

What can you do today?

Take control of the sales training for your staff today. Research and find a good sales trainer or talk to your business associates or mentors to get a recommendation.

Do you make it easy for people to buy from you?

This is another one of those tips that seems to be obvious but many businesses struggle with the concept. They have adopted overly complicated procedures that make buying anything a nightmare. They don't take credit cards, they are hard to get to, they don't have enough sales staff, you have to order products and wait weeks for them to arrive— all in all they just seem to miss the point.

If you want your business to develop a reputation for being magnificent, make it as easy as possible for your customers to buy your products. If you don't they will go to somewhere that does.

The key word here is 'simple'. Keep it simple, in every possible way. To do this you need to be a keen observer of how your sales system works. Is it streamlined?

Is it set up to be convenient for you but not for your customers?

Look at everything you do - all from a customer's perspective with the one overriding objective being ease of buying or booking.

I often hear business owners saying they don't take some credit cards because the merchant rates are too high. Put your prices up to cover the costs and accept the credit cards. Think about the last time you went to a business and they wouldn't accept the credit card you wanted to use. It was an inconvenience and an irritation. Your customers expect to use their preferred particular credit card and if you don't accept it they are likely to go elsewhere. You can even take payments on mobile phones. Research and take a look at what is available.

What difficulties have you encountered in the buying process and would you go back to the business where you were confronted with the problem?

What can you do today?

Look at your business and try to find one way to make it easier for your customers to buy from you. Often that is all it takes. If you don't take credit cards you really do need to. Ring your local bank and get the process in motion.

How you sold yesterday may not apply to how you sell today or tomorrow

Customers are changing and their needs and expectations are changing constantly. How this affects customer service has been discussed in a previous section but it is worth discussing how it affects selling.

It is easy for a business to fall into the trap of creating a rigid sales process so that everyone who sells follows the same format. In fact this is generally a good process, but if the process is not reviewed on a regular basis you may start to lose customers. As the customers' needs and expectations change, the sales process you use will need to be modified.

Imagine how butchers had to change how they sold beef in the United Kingdom after the mad cow disease outbreak. It would have been different to the way they did it before.

This is obviously an extreme example but look at how travel is sold these days. The words 'safe destination' are now well and truly implanted in the sales pitch for most holiday destinations, a concept we were aware of but not as an everyday accepted risk assessment for when we plan our holidays as it has become today.

The point I am trying to make is that we need to review how we sell our products and services on a regular basis. There is really no room for the old, 'That's the way we always did it' mentality. Sales are dynamic and ever changing, regardless of the business. It is the customers who drive sales and the more flexible and adaptable your business the greater your chances of succeeding where others fail.

What can you do today?

Today is the day to review your sales process to see if you have become a little set in your ways. If you have, turn it upside down and breathe some life in to it. But just do it.

Become a sales analyser—every time you put your hand in your pocket

To become better at selling you need to become a better observer of how other businesses do it. Every time you make a purchase start reviewing the way you were sold. Look for the good and the bad. Take the good observations and, if you can, incorporate them into your own business. Remember I said some of the best business owners are observers?

Because we are so used to going into various businesses and making a purchase it is easy to go through the process on auto pilot. But if you start to become more observant it can be very interesting. You start to notice a lot more; you can sense when a sale is lost by the salesperson or when the sale is made.

Standing in a queue can have some benefits - not many I might add - but it does give you time to watch what's happening. Call it free market research.

I enjoy it a lot more when there is a good salesperson at work. It is interesting to see how they develop a rapport with the customer, ask the right questions, listen to the answers and respond accordingly.

When you do become an observer it helps if you are a little prepared. I talk about keeping a notebook handy elsewhere in this manual and this is one of those situations when it will come in handy. As soon as you see something, good or bad, that strikes a chord make a note of it and refer to it later.

After a while you will collect a lot of valuable information that could be beneficial to your business.

What can you do today?

Next time you go into a business to buy something observe how they handle the sale. Do they simply take your money or do they actually sell their products to you?
Try and do this every time you buy something this week and you will be surprised at how much information you take in and the tips you pick up.

How do you monitor your sales?

All businesses monitor the money coming in - it is the lifeblood of the business - and cash flow is one of those areas that always need attention. But when it comes to monitoring sales, businesses generally pay less attention to detail.

If you sell only one product for a fixed amount it is pretty easy to figure out how many you sold at the end of the - trading day. Few businesses, however, have this level of simplicity. You need to pay particular attention to what you are selling or, more importantly, what isn't selling and why. Sales reports can be simple one-page documents kept beside the cash register to be filled in whenever a sale is made. Better than this is a clever cash register that breaks the sales down according to pre-determined categories. As long as your team press the right keys the information should be pretty accurate.

Regardless of how you monitor your sales, the information collected needs to be reviewed and ideally compared to the last week, last month and even last year. This way you start to develop a greater feel for any sales trends that happen within your business. This is very valuable information as it allows you to develop a much more strategic approach to selling. Larger organisations (and also a lot of smaller ones) have very detailed sales reports. They know the value of understanding what is selling and what isn't within a business.

The bottom line is that the more control and understanding you have of the products and services you sell the more likely you are to develop a sustainable business. It takes the hit-and-miss factor out of the equation.

What can you do today?

How can you improve your sales monitoring process within your business?
Is it time to upgrade your cash till or buy some new software to give you the right answers?
If you don't have a system put one in place today- start with a simple form beside your cash till.

What is the customer's main concern in the sales process?

As a customer our biggest concerns when it comes to buying are whether the product we buy will not work as it should, whether we are paying too much for it or if it breaks we will have thrown our money away. If you can dispel these concerns of your customers you will be well and truly on the way to increasing sales.

So, how do you dispel these concerns?

Let's look at the first one first - the product not working as it should. Clearly you need to tell the customer that if for any reason they are not satisfied with the way the product works they can bring it back and either exchange it or get a refund (depending on your policy).

If there are conditions let them know in advance, don't make it a surprise.

If they are concerned about paying too much, explain your pricing policy and if you are more expensive than other places explain why. Perhaps you have better after-sales service. Maybe the products are slightly different. Or your business is smaller than the competitors and while you may not have the buying power you make up for it with more personalised service. Give the customer the facts and let them make their own decision. For long-term repeat business it is much better to be up front than to let the customer find out for themselves and feel ripped off. Finally, explain how your guarantee system works. Be specific and make sure the customer is clear on the life of the guarantee and what it covers. If it doesn't have a guarantee, explain why. Some products don't and there is a legitimate reason for this. If you buy a goldfish and it dies you are unlikely to be able to get a refund.

By addressing the above in a few short sentences, the customer's concerns are alleviated and they should be happy to buy the product. When was the last time you had someone explain away your concerns in that manner? Probably not recently but if you do it in your business, you will soon be classified as one of the winning ones.

What can you do today?

What are you doing to remove concerns that your customers may have regarding buying your products? Think about how you will answer those concerns and make sure your staff can answer the customers' concerns accurately as well. Try it—you will be amazed at the results.

Always ask for the sale

The last and most fatal sales mistake is quite simply not asking for the sale. This means being prepared to ask the customer for their business and it is often described as the point when most sales are lost. The salesperson can go through the whole process, but they simply don't ask for the business at the end.

What does 'ask for the sale' actually mean? It means asking the customer if they would like to buy the item you are selling and it really is that simple. This is that awkward moment when the customer is deciding if they want to make the purchase or not. If the salesperson is standing there waiting expectantly, often the customer will walk away from the sale simply because they feel under pressure to make a decision.

I have a lot of sales reps coming to my business to sell various products. I sit through presentation after presentation and then most of them just pack up and leave without even asking me if we can do business together. By asking the customer if they would like to buy the product you are not being pushy—you are simply trying to help them to make a decision. Clearly it would be better for the business if they did buy the product but they can still say no at this stage.
Be prepared to ask for the sale.

What can you do today?

Do you and your staff ask for the sale?
If not, why not?
What is the barrier stopping this from happening? Is it a simple matter to correct?

If you are not sure how to handle it revert back to getting a professional sales trainer to come and help you work it out.

CHAPTER 9
QUESTION EVERYTHING – CONSTANTLY

Having an open and inquisitive mind is probably the most powerful asset any budding entrepreneur can have. Business is not static these days, it is changing constantly, it is exciting, it is challenging and we all need to be striving to keep up and hopefully lead the way in this environment. To truly stand a chance at becoming successful you need to be able to honestly appraise what you are doing every day and look for ways to do it better. You can't sit back and be content that your business will be just as successful in the coming years as it has been in the past few years if you don't review and modify what you do.

You need to question everything you do and you need to question it regularly.

I love this about experienced entrepreneurs—they are not afraid to ask anyone for an opinion about what they do or for a suggestion to make their business better. In this section we are going to be looking at how to question everything you do.

In this section we will cover:

- Without this there is no point asking questions
- Question your business partners—ask them to be honest

- Walk around your business—and really look at everything
- Go to successful businesses and find out why they are successful
- Mystery shop your way to success
- Do you charge enough?
- If it doesn't feel right it probably isn't—the business owner's sixth sense
- Talk to your staff—ask them for ideas and their opinions
- Don't be afraid to be a manager—sometimes it's tough
- Write your own operations manual as a way to question what you do

Without this there is no point asking questions

This section covers the importance of being able to question and review everything you do in your business. If you are not prepared to accept what you find out or to do something about it, don't bother asking the question.

Many business owners are rigid and set in their ways. They think they want to hear about their business from their customers but what they want to hear is just the good stuff—they don't want to know about any negatives and, often, they can get quite hostile.

It is a real sign of business maturity to be able to take constructive criticism on board and use it to make your business even better. Think about it, how grateful would you be if someone's honesty gave you the opportunity to make your business better?

Businesses that operate as if they are set in stone are dinosaurs and many can't survive in the modern business environment where the need to change and evolve is here to stay. Ask lots of questions of the people you deal with on a regular basis. If you ask the questions, have an open mind about the answers. You have to make the final decision about what you will do with the information.

What can you do today?

Do you have an open mind to constructive criticism? How do you respond if someone tells you something not so flattering about your business?

If you do have an open mind great—ask more people for their opinions and recommendations and use the information wisely. If you don't it's time to work on opening up and becoming more flexible. Think about constructive criticism or feedback about your business as an exceptional opportunity and be sincerely grateful to the people giving you this feedback.

Question your business partners—ask them to be honest

In this instance I would consider business partners to mean anyone you have a relationship with- your professional advisers (lawyer, accountant), your suppliers, friends in business, your business mentors and really anyone else who is in a position to know about your business.

Just as we have discussed the importance of asking your customers for their feedback and their recommendations to improve your business, your business partners can offer excellent advice from a different perspective. An open-minded business owner has access to a lot of good information and advice from their network of business partners—all you have to do to access this network is to ask.

Look for ways to run your business better, for successful marketing ideas, for new products and services and for ways to attract more customers. Just one good idea from a business partner could be a significant turning point for your business but you have to be big enough to ask. Often it can be interesting to see the different perspective your business partners bring to your business. They will have different views and ideas developed from being involved in their own industries and businesses and their opinions and ideas really may be things you would not have even considered.

Sitting down with a business partner and asking them how you could make your business better is a little tough and it puts them on the spot. I suggest making a small list of topics that might include things such as customer service, product range, sales, advertising and business appearance and so on. Use this list to guide the conversation. This also gives you an opportunity to write their responses. If you do this exercise with ten business partners you might start to see some common themes emerging.

Be prepared to ask your business partners for their ideas and recommendations.

Most will give their honest opinions freely but, remember, if you ask for them be prepared to listen.

What can you do today?

Make up a list of the areas of your business that you would like to discuss and then pick one business partner per day for the next week to ask for their opinions and feedback on how you could make your business better.

Walk around your business—and really look at everything

When you visit the same place every day, year after year, it is very easy to walk in and out with blinkers on. Throughout this manual I have made the recommendation that you stop what you are doing and go and really look at certain aspects of your business - whether it is your front entrance, your signage, your staff and your customers, whatever. Well, this idea is really to reinforce that message.

You need to become more observant in your business. You need to not only look more closely at every aspect of your business but also to be able to make changes that will improve the business.

As a business grows it is easy for the owners to lose touch with a lot of the every day events going on. While it becomes impossible and in some ways unproductive for the business owner to know all of the nuts and bolts it is important for them to have a clear understanding of how things work. The more they understand the more they can look for ways to make things run better.

You need to get out of your work space and just walk around. Clear your head. Open your eyes and try to look at the business without your normal blinkers on. Talk to your staff, talk to some customers. Go across the road and look at your business, have a good look at your website, read through your own brochure and look at the products that you have on display.

There are so many aspects of the business that need to be reviewed on a constant basis that it can be daunting. The first step is to remove the blinkers and open your mind to becoming an observer. After a week of doing this it will become second nature. The habit of walking in and out of your business with blinkers on has probably formed over many years.

Once you become a keen observer you can then start to make the business even better—and that can take it from mediocrity to magnificence.

What can you do today?

Stand up and take a walk around your business and really look at it. Often you will be amazed by the things you see that you hadn't noticed before. It is all about shifting your perceptions and opening up the mind.

The benefits for you will be that your business will improve by you paying attention to the smaller details.

Go to successful businesses and find out why they are successful

This is good advice and again it is along the theme of becoming an excellent business observer. Whenever you find out about a really successful business, perhaps they have won an award or your family and friends are talking about them or there may have been an article in the newspaper, I suggest you pay the business a visit.

What they sell really doesn't matter; how they run the business does?
What makes it so successful?
Why do people keep coming back?

Why does it win awards?

So you need to go in armed (metaphorically speaking of course) to find out their secrets and to see if you can apply any of them to your business. Often finding out why a business does so well is not clearly obvious on first inspection.

From my own experience, it is more the way they do business rather than any one specific detail. It is the attitude of the staff, it is the attention to detail and it is the inviting and welcoming feel of the business. Rarely is it their pricing, a misconception that many business owners are far too preoccupied with.

Becoming a good observer of anything takes time, training and effort. But it starts with opening your eyes.

A quick walk around a successful business might give you a few clues but you need to really go a little deeper. Give them a call and make an enquiry about their product.

Consider how they handle it. Most importantly, after the call did you feel like going to this business? Take the time to get to know that business, listen to their sales staff, make a purchase and see how the transaction is handled, or ask a few difficult questions. Whatever you do, try to get a very good feeling for the business.

Make a list of what you feel makes this business so good at what it does and beside each of the points indicate if they could be applied to your business. Then set about implementing them.

What can you do today?

We all know about those businesses that seem to be considered the best at what they do (hopefully it's yours). Well, find one and pay it a visit. Go there with your observer's hat on and try to clearly identify what makes them so good at what they do.

Mystery shop your way to success

Mystery shoppers are used by more businesses every day to provide an independent evaluation of what the business is doing well and what it could be doing better. They are not witch hunts trying to find the underachieving employee who can then be thrown to the wolves. They are mechanisms for giving an honest appraisal of a business. Companies that offer mystery shopping services can be found in most cities.

Often this is a service provided by marketing companies and training organisations.

In more recent times, firms that do nothing but offer customer service evaluations, utilising mystery shoppers as one of their key resources, are being set up.
Ideally no one, not even the business owner, will know when a mystery shopper will be dropping by. They will appear just like any other customer and that is the aim. A short while later, a report will be issued and the overall performance of the business can be measured. Periodically the mystery shopper evaluation can be repeated to determine if the business has improved or worsened.

Normally the first mystery shopper is the tough one. It highlights the most glaring weaknesses and it can be quite confronting for the business owners and the staff. Often the initial response is to point the finger and blame, which is not the best course of action. What is needed following this first report is a clear and level-headed plan to rectify any problems and to work at improving the business in any of the areas that need improving.

Mystery shoppers can be used to evaluate the following:

• Service and selling skills offered over the telephone
• How easy the business is to find
• How appealing the entrance is
• General layout of the business
• First impressions
• Overall cleanliness of the business
• Overall ambience of the business (smells, sounds etc.)
• Appearance of the staff
• Selling skills of the staff
• Perceived value for money
• General level of customer service
• Quality of the products or services sold.

There are many other related and specific areas of any business that can be evaluated and the information is usually valuable. While it can be a little confronting the end result is that your business will have the opportunity to rectify problems that can be losing you customers.

It is also interesting to note that if your team knows you are having regular mystery shoppers they tend to try a little harder as they never quite know if the customer standing in front of them is today's mystery shopper. Because of this, it is important to share any mystery shopper findings, good and bad, with the team. Show them the information that is collected and that you are doing something with it.

It takes a strong business to use mystery shoppers - but they are a great way to work out the difference between mediocre and winning.

What can you do today?

Can you use mystery shopper evaluations to build your business? If you can, why not arrange one today?

Do you charge enough?

Pricing is a tough subject—do you charge too much or too little?

There are a lot of businesses that simply don't charge enough, making it really difficult to ever make the business successful. I received some very good advice when I was starting out in my business life—a very successful friend and entrepreneur sat me down and said, 'Someone has to be the most expensive and it may as well be you. But if you are going to be the most expensive you have to be the best at what you do. Your business has to shine in every way.' An interesting concept and one I have tried to adhere to in any business I have run.

I believe customers are less concerned with pricing as they are with service and value for money. Sure there are a lot of businesses that operate in price conscious markets. But even in these markets I believe the same principle applies—people will pay more for quality.

If your business runs on tight margins it is hard to make it magnificent as so much energy has to be focused on just making ends meet. If you can gradually build your prices up with the aim being to offer better service and better experience to your customers, in general it will pay off.

Charging what you are worth is a hard concept for a lot of people. They charge what they think their customers are prepared to pay and often the two are a long way apart. If your business doesn't make enough money it will not be successful, simple as that. If you are just scraping by and not really getting ahead in your business, maybe you are simply not charging enough.

Winning businesses are not afraid to charge what they are worth because they can back it up by being the best at what they do.

What can you do today?

Today is a good day to review what you charge. Look at all of your pricing and see if you can charge more and deliver a better product and a higher level of service.

If it doesn't feel right it probably isn't—the business owner's sixth sense

I have spoken about the business owner's sixth sense with a lot of entrepreneurs and I have experienced it myself many times. It is the ability to be able to tell intuitively that something is not right in your business; it is the ability to be able to sense that something is wrong with a proposed deal or the person sitting across the desk from you who is saying something you don't quite believe. It most certainly exists, and those aware of it use it to their advantage. They encourage this sixth sense to grow and they listen when it needs to be heard.

This sense develops over time and it is just as relevant in life as it is in business.

We need to learn to listen to this little voice at the back of our mind. Any time I have ignored it, it has either cost me money or caused me grief.

This is one of those tips where I am sure some readers will assume I have lost the plot but I have no doubt many will know exactly what I am talking about.

There are many intangible aspects of running a business that have as much impact and bearing on succeeding as the more tangible and real aspects.

Have you ever been in a situation in your business when it just doesn't feel right but you ignore the nagging feeling and go ahead anyway only to find out it was a bad decision? Well that tingling wasn't your 'spider-sense'. It was your business owner's sixth sense trying to get out and to be heard. It is a priceless tool that will help you as an entrepreneur to be far more successful and enjoy your business if you let it.

What can you do today?

From today, try to listen to your business owner's sixth sense.
When you have nagging doubts try to decide whether it is just fear or natural caution or is it more of a gut feeling coming from within. The more you listen to your sixth sense the more it will talk to you.

Talk to your staff—ask them for ideas and their opinions

Many businesses take an almost us-and-them approach to their staff. For most of us, life without staff would be pretty hard. Our businesses would never be able to grow, our workloads would be enormous and there would be a hollow feeling when it comes to sharing the trials and tribulations experienced in our daily business life.

Involve your team in your business. Ask them for their ideas and their opinions; after all, they often know your business almost as well if not better than you. Most certainly they will know the specific jobs they do better than you.

The more you let your staff play an active role in your business the more they will grow, the more ideas they will come up with and ultimately the better your business will run and the more successful it will be.

Involving your staff means asking for their opinions and thoughts. It means taking these opinions and thoughts seriously and being appreciative of the fact that your staff members are prepared to be involved. Just because you give them a weekly pay packet doesn't mean they have to open up; it is a real trust situation and it needs to be well handled.

Just as I talked previously about the importance of treating your customers with respect, I think you should have the same level of respect for your staff. Sure, there will always be times when you drive each other crazy or make mistakes but you are working on the same team.

Get your staff involved in your business. Ask them for their thoughts and opinions and build a strong relationship based on mutual respect.

What can you do today?

What is your attitude towards your staff?
Is it us-and-them or have you got a team?

Do you ask your staff for their input on running your business and do you take their advice seriously?
Write a simple paragraph about your views about your relationship with your staff and how you would like to see it evolve.

Don't be afraid to be a manager- sometimes it's tough

Being a manager is a big task. It covers an enormous amount of ground and it is constantly changing. Being a manager means being a leader, it means being a decision maker and it means being committed to what you do. As a business owner you fall into the role of being a manager by default and sometimes that can be the hardest part of running your business. You know how to do your business but you may never have had to manage people before so it is a whole new ball game.

Being a manager sometimes means making tough decisions. Sometimes, staff just 'don't work out' and they have to be dismissed. You have to make decisions that affect the lives of others. There is a balance between what is best for the individual and what is best for the business. Remember that many people study for years to become business managers.

Having commitment to becoming a better manager starts in your own head.

Sure you will make mistakes, but as long as you learn from them your skills will improve. Understanding and accepting the complexity of being a manager is one part, but realising you are not expected to know everything overnight is the real key to becoming a good manager.

Read books on management styles and ideas—there are an amazing number around. Do a management course and ask your mentors for their ideas and advice. You will become a better manager for it, which is very rewarding personally, and your business will benefit from your increased ability as a manager.

What can you do today?

If you are in the position where you need to be a manager make a commitment today to be the best manager you can be.

Enrol in a managerial course or buy a book about being a better manager.

Treat it like learning any new skill.

Write your own operations manual as a way to question what you do

An operations manual is simply a written description of how your business operates on a daily basis. You should have one, regardless of the size of the business. Operations manuals put details in black and white and writing one is the perfect way to question why you do things in a particular way.

An operations manual can be as complex or as simple as you want it to be. It is going to be used internally by other members of your team, not put on display for the general public to read. It should outline how any situation should be processed within your business; for example:

• The opening procedures for the business
• Expectations regarding staff appearance and conduct

- Customer service procedures
- Processing sales
- Handling complaints
- ordering stock
- Paying accounts
- Company policy on staff entitlements
- Use of company vehicles
- Cleaning within the business.

The list really is endless and clearly it depends on the type of business you run.

Writing a manual like this really does make you investigate every part of your business in a detailed manner. Having written a few and advised my clients to write them the same feedback comes out every time—writing an operations manual is a work in progress.

As you start writing a section, you start thinking about how it works and come up with better ideas on the spot. So the end product is helpful for making sure everyone knows what to do within your business but the writing process is great for questioning what you do and coming up with ways to do things better.

What can you do today?

If you haven't got an operations manual today is the day to start it. First, make a list of all of the operational aspects of your business and then start filling in the details. Accept the manual will be a work in progress. If you have an operations manual already, determine whether it is current and still accurate. Pull it out and read it cover to cover; I am sure you will make changes for the better.

CHAPTER 10
BECOME THE ULTIMATE CORPORATE CITIZEN

As business owners and entrepreneurs we make our living from the community where we live and work. I believe very strongly that it is important to give as much back to your community as you can. This needs to be done in a sincere way; not in the anticipation of receiving accolades or acknowledgment. If you do get recognition, accept it with pride—it is okay to be told you have done something good.

From my observations those businesses that are great corporate citizens deserve every success that comes their way. There are multitudes of ways in which a business can be a good corporate citizen and these are covered in this section.

What's covered in this section:

- Be involved in the community where you do business
- Look for opportunities outside of the normal
- Stand up and be counted
- Share your knowledge and experience with others
- Encourage your staff to be good corporate citizens
- Some things can't be measured in pounds and pence
- Invest in the future of your industry

- Don't be afraid to tell people you are a good corporate citizen
- Make up a plan to make you the ultimate corporate citizen

Be involved in the community where you do business

First and foremost we have to start at the beginning and that simply means getting involved. Every community has a host of organisations where people give their time freely to get behind good causes that need some help. They may be charities, they may be environmental groups, and they may be groups trying to improve conditions for particular members of the community. The choice is up to you. If you have a particular passion, use it to get involved.

Who has the spare time to get involved in community-based groups?

Generally none of us but typically the people I meet who are doing the most in their community are the busiest of all. They run their own businesses, manage their families, try to find time for themselves and yet they still get involved.

Why?

Because it makes them feel good.

If you can't find the time to get involved yourself, support community groups with the products or services your business offers. Donate money to them or let them use your facilities to help raise money.

I choose two or three special events to offer my services free of charge every year. This means that at any one time we will have a project we are working on that is community based. I am happy to cover the cost of this and my team get behind it as well. We all feel great and to be honest the events have a greater chance of succeeding if they have access to professional event management and fundraising advice.

Whatever level of involvement you can offer, embrace the community where you live and run your business and play an active role in making it a better place for everyone living there.

What can you do today?

How involved are you in your community?
A lot or not at all?

 If you are involved a lot you can sit this one out—you deserve the break.

If you're not involved at all today is the day to get involved. Talk to your staff about what you would like to do and ask for their suggestions on how you could get more involved in your community. It might be something as simple as sponsoring a junior sporting team or it may be ambitious, such as raising a pile of money to build a facility for disabled people.

Look for opportunities outside of the normal

Trying to decide how to get involved in your community can be quite challenging as there are so many opportunities; however, there are always some opportunities that are a little less obvious but equally worthy.

A while back I knew someone who used to work for a local bus company.

This guy read in the paper that the local blood bank was having trouble getting office workers to donate blood. A little research showed that the main cause was the time it took for the workers to leave the office, have some lunch, get to the blood bank, donate and then get back to work. It just took too long. So he spoke to bosses who not only offered to put on a special bus service where the workers could eat their lunch on the way to the blood bank, but then did a recruitment drive for blood within its own employees. They guaranteed to have them back at work within an hour and in a short amount of time they had nearly doubled the amount of donors.

What can you do today?

Look for problems in the community and see if you can offer a solution. It may not be as big and bold as some community based projects but to the people involved it is equally as important. Plus it is a rewarding experience to be able to solve a problem yourself. Read the newspapers, listen to the news and look for problems where your business could help provide a solution.

Stand up and be counted

When you get caught up in your own business it is easy to start to break your life into two very distinct halves—the business half and the non-business half.

The business half can easily become the biggest part, after all you have a lot riding on it and you are enthused and passionate about what you do. While this is happening, you need to keep playing a role in the other areas of your life.

Business owners are generally respected in the community. People understand they give a lot back to the community, they provide jobs and they make the economy go round. For this reason their opinions are valued. This makes it very important for business owners to play an active role in the running of their community.

When there are important issues being debated in your community have your say. Voice your opinion and don't be afraid to be a little controversial. It is easy to say nothing in case you might offend a customer who has a different opinion but it is more important to stand up for injustice or the things within your community worth fighting for.

When you have your own business don't stop being a part of the community where you live. Write a letter, voice your opinion, call the local radio station - whatever it takes just play a role.

What can you do today?

Have you become an observer of your community or do you play an active role?
If it's been a while since you were able to get passionate about things you disagree with in your community maybe today is the day to redirect some of your business passion back into the place you call home.

Share your knowledge and experience with others

Helping other businesses to grow and succeed is a worthy community activity.

You can offer to share your experiences at a business gathering or even a presentation at a school. It is surprising how many of these organisations struggle to find interesting people to share their knowledge and experiences.

Take on a work experience student in your office. Give them the opportunity to see if they like the industry you are in. Think back to when you did something similar and how you found it benefited you. But don't wait for the schools to contact you, give them a call yourself and let them know you are interested in taking on work experience students.

Coach a sporting team. There are never enough parents to get behind local sporting teams. Introduce what you have learned about leadership and team spirit to a group of kids wanting to play sport.

Run a free seminar about something you know about—maybe running your own business. If you have managed to survive for a while you are suitably qualified to share your views with others.

Whatever interest grabs you, being prepared to share your knowledge and experience is a good way to become a better corporate citizen.

What can you do today?

Make up a list of ways you can share your knowledge and experience with other people in your local community. Then get on the telephone and turn the list into reality.

Encourage your staff to be good corporate citizens

If you're prepared to be a good corporate citizen, your colleagues will be more likely to want to get involved as well. Make it easy for them to do this and encourage them to participate. It is important not to be threatening or intimidating—some people just don't want to get involved and that is fine. They should not feel like their job is not secure if they don't.

What you are trying to do is to provide the right environment for your staff to feel they would like to get involved. This may mean making a few allowances for them giving up their time, it may even mean some financial support; for example, if a group of your staff want to enter a fun run, offer to sponsor them.

Community involvement is a great team building exercise and it is rewarding in a lot of ways—not the least of which is the realisation that as an individual you can really make a difference. Provide the right working environment and most workplaces will automatically produce some community minded individuals who will drive the process from within. Encourage and support them as much as you feel able and recognise their efforts.

What can you do today?

Are there ways where you could be more encouraging of your staff to help them become better corporate citizens? Why not get your team in and ask them?
If you already have a proactive team who are heavily involved in the community can you acknowledge their efforts more?

Some things can't be measured in pounds and pence

In every business plan I write I always make a point of encouraging the business to become more involved in their community. I outline the importance of being a good corporate citizen and the fact that consumers these days want to deal with businesses actively involved in their community.

Some business owners just don't get it. They ask questions like, "How much free publicity will I get?" or, "How many new customers will it get me?" or, "How much will this add to my bottom line?" Some things simply can't be measured in pounds and pence and community involvement is certainly one of those things.

I can't tell you how much more money it will make you, but I can tell you there are a lot of consumers out there making conscious decisions about where they will spend their money. Given the choice between spending it on a business that plays an active role in the community and one that doesn't, what choice do you think they will make? Apart from that concept alone—what about doing the right thing and having integrity. You need to think much deeper than just returns on investment. Even the largest organisations in the world have realised this and they are going to great lengths to show the world both corporate compassion and corporate responsibility.

This is why I have no problem with businesses that promote themselves as being actively involved in their community; in fact I recommend they do. If it means the community wins, that is all that matters. We are all charged with the responsibility of making the world a better place.

What can you do today?

If you find yourself asking questions about returns on investment when it comes to helping to build a better community you need to develop a measuring system other than money. Call it karma or whatever you like and accept this is as equally relevant a currency as money, and in many ways it is much better.

Invest in the future of your industry

Investing your time, energy and even possibly some money into the future of your industry is another part of being a good corporate citizen. Clearly it is different to helping a charity or another community based organisation but it is just as important.

One example I can talk about is a relationship I have with two local schools.

They have a good business courses with a strong bent towards marketing. I'm regularly giving guest lectures, simply because my teachers couldn't inspire the skin off a rice pudding. I gladly give my time freely as I believe very strongly in putting back into my industry and also providing assistance to the next generation coming through. Too much is put on the shoulders of academia. Telling people reality is just as important and educational.

Too many people have a 'What's in it for me?' approach to business. Truly successful people are always prepared to give of themselves as they understand the big picture.

What can you do today?

The very next time you read about someone who has gone out of their way to help make your community a better place do some detective work and track down their address and send them a card or a thank you letter.

Don't be afraid to tell people you are a good corporate citizen

Just as I feel it is important to be a good corporate citizen I certainly don't see anything wrong with telling people you are. Put the certificates on the wall in a public place. Include what you do in your company profile or on your website.

Larger organisations actually make up entire brochures showing what they do in their community and, again, I don't think there is anything wrong with doing this.

As explained earlier in this section, consumers want to deal with companies that are good corporate citizens and it is up to the business to let them know.

Don't be afraid to blow your own trumpet and say you are actively involved in your community- it is something to be proud of, not embarrassed about.

Don't think it is just about big things either. Donate a few pounds to a local charity. It is as significant as a big donation. Giving too much may cause your business to get into financial difficulties, which does no good to anyone. Get involved at a level you can manage easily, both financially and time wise.

Do what you can and be prepared to let your customers know what you do.

They will appreciate it and you for making their community a better place to live, regardless of the size of your contribution.

What can you do today?

How do you let your customers know that you play an active role in the community?

Today is the day to put the certificate on the wall or include your community involvement on your website or in your promotional material.

Make up a plan to make you the ultimate corporate citizen

Like any component of a successful business, the better you plan the greater your chances of succeeding. The same principle applies to the goal of becoming the ultimate corporate citizen. Making up a plan for how you and your business will play an active role in your community is a wise choice of action.

This plan should address:

• Which types of organisations you would like to get involved with
• How much time each week you can spare
• How much financial support you can afford to give
• What products and services you offer (remembering, they still have cost)
• Ways to encourage your staff to get involved
• Specific details about how you will tell your customers you are community spirited
• How you will recognise other people in the community who get involved
• How you can share your own knowledge and experience.

This doesn't need to be a big and in-depth plan, just a few pages addressing each of the questions above. Start a file called 'Becoming the Ultimate Corporate Citizen' and you are well and truly on your way to achieving this goal. Once you have your plan in place, take the time to share it with your staff. They will, after all, be playing an important role.

CHAPTER 11
MAKE YOURSELF AS IMPRESSIVE AS YOUR BUSINESS

When running a business of any size or in any industry it is easy to focus all your attention on the business and not a lot on yourself. The people I have encountered, who have built amazing businesses, all invest as much in themselves as they do in their businesses. This doesn't just mean financially; it means energy, it means personal development, it means helping others to grow.

Putting all of your resources into your business is an easy trap, one I have certainly fallen into in the past. When you start to balance your life the results are often quite astonishing. Your business thrives and so does your life. You enjoy what you do a lot more. Your decisions are better and you portray a feeling of success that attracts success into your life. This chapter will look at ways to help you to become as impressive as your business.

This section will cover:

- Appearances are everything
- Have a strong moral code—with no shades of grey
- Be a fair negotiator
- Be more than your business
- Have a life outside of your business
- Be a supporter of other business associates
- Mix with people you can learn from

- Make decisions—procrastination is a killer
- Commit to improving your business skills daily
- Don't be a victim (and keep people who play victim out of your life)

Appearances are everything

Appearances are everything is an old saying which, from my own experience, I don't think is necessarily 100 per cent correct but I have no doubt that appearances are very important. In my dealings with successful entrepreneurs they generally look the part. They have an air of confidence about them and they feel successful.

I had this drummed into me at an early age. If you want to succeed at what you do you need to look the part: dress appropriately, be groomed appropriately, and drive an appropriate car and so on. If you are trying to portray yourself as a successful business owner, make yourself look successful.

Think back to the last time you walked into a business that looked like it was on skid row. Not very inspiring, was it? You certainly don't get a feeling of confidence from a business like this. The same can apply to an individual. If you want your customers to have confidence in you then look the part. This applies not only to you but to anyone representing your business.

Uniforms should always be neat and tidy, well ironed and of course clean.

Company vehicles should be well maintained and clean. Crumpled, worn-out uniforms and beaten up company cars send a clear message: business is either struggling or the owners just don't care—both normally go hand in hand.

I recently pulled up at a set of traffic lights and waiting next to me was one of the most beat up and filthy cars I had seen in a long time. Clouds of smoke were billowing out from the engine and the driver was choking back a cigarette.

All over this car were signs promoting a particular business. A business which I gather owned the car.

They were selling the virtues of filtered water as a means of living a healthier life. There is no way I would ever buy filtered water from this company. If their vehicle is like this, what must their end product be like?

In the same vein, have you ever seen those cars promoting an 'extra income' working from home? I've always wondered whether it was worth it as they were driving a 'Y' registration Vauxhall Vectra in dirty green.

We all make these assumptions based on appearances. To succeed at what you do look the part and your customers will know that you take your business seriously.

So to give you some idea of why wearing the right clothes and colour are important I asked blogger, writer, designer and all round fashion expert Tanisha Degutis*, (@TanishaDegutis) to give a few tips. You'll notice at the beginning of the book where we talk about the psychology of colours, the same process applies to the clothes you and your colleagues wear.

Black - This colour will make your outfit and general image look stricter and put together. This is not always a good idea though, because it can create slightly distant atmosphere. Black is more suitable for special occasions, evening meetings and etc...

Light blue - A colour that will create a trustworthy impression. A baby blue shirt will make you look younger and can even take 10 years of your shoulders. This colour can create a youthful, laid back look.

Dark blue - A good option. Wearing this colour suit will make your face look brighter, which will come in handy if you are having long meetings that day. It's also known as the colour that doesn't sit in people's memory for long, so you will be able to wear a dark blue suit a few times a week. Just switch your shirt colours. So in other words, it'll be a good return on investment by being worn many times in a given period. Dark blue is also known as the colour of wisdom and seriousness. This shade of blue is a must in your wardrobe if you are businessman or a businesswoman.

Grey - It's a warmer colour, which makes it a great choice if you are seeking to make people feel more comfortable around you. It helps surrounding people to open up to you a little more.

When choosing suits, go for dark grey, it will always look more expensive then light grey, even if it's a cheaper price range.

Pink or baby pink - This is another great colour to bring out youthfulness and creates a laid back atmosphere in the room. Baby pink is a "sweet", soft colour and sometimes can create a 'naive bimbo' image. I wouldn't recommend this colour for businesswoman of any kind. But having a baby pink shirt in a businessman's closet is a must. It will come in handy at unofficial meetings, employee parties, etc...

Purple - From past centuries this colour was known as the symbol of royalty and luxury. It was hard to produce, so only very rich people could afford wearing purple clothes. This colour was always associated with royalty and highly respected people.

Light purple / Orchid would look appropriate if you work in the office and would add some brightness to your complexion.

Dark purple jacket would create a serious polished look. I would strongly recommend wearing different shades of purple, especially if you work in creative environment.

Green - This is a must have colour in your wardrobe if you work in a stressful environment or if your work is directly related to finances (bank, finance department, etc.). Green relieves tiredness and can help you feel more energetic. Light green can help create a youthful, playful and relaxed look. It is a great colour to wear if you work in a relaxed, creative surrounding. Be careful when choosing it if you work in serious environment. It can make you look too playful and not put together.
Dark green is a must colour for those with conservative outlooks. It brings in seriousness to the whole image.

Red – I highly recommend warmer tones of red on the days when you need / want to be in the centre of attention. Especially on the days when you are running a meeting or doing a speech. Red will embrace your confidence and will make you feel more energetic.

I wouldn't recommend wearing red from head to toes. It can irritate people who surround you. One red item per look will do. Two - if you are brave. Three - if you are a woman (lipstick, bag or shoes do count).

Brown - It's perfect for meetings with a new client. It's a warm and soft colour that creates a trustworthy impression. You will look like a reliable and practical person with a good reputation by wearing a brown suit.

Brown is a colour associated with wisdom and stability. I would suggest having a brown suit for any type of business person. It's a good option when creating a new business relationship.

White - It's a clean, weightless colour that can create a smooth and bright look without any eye irritation. White clothes will always look festive. This is a good colour to go for if you want to be in the centre of attention. A white suit or jacket will do the deed. It will create a polished look with a fresh bright twist. It will make you stand out from the crowd.

I wouldn't recommend wearing a white suit or white top together on a daily basis. Wear it occasionally or for important days like signing a contract with new partners or an employee motivational meeting. It will make you stand out from the crowd and will help you exude positivity.
A white shirt can be worn on a daily basis, but can be a little boring if it's your only choice from day to day.

What can you do today?

Make a list of five ways you can improve either your appearance or the appearance of some aspects of your business and action them. It might mean buying some new clothes, or getting uniforms or having the company car detailed.

Have a strong moral code—with no shades of grey

How many examples do you know of high-profile people who were shining stars but became corporate disgraces? It really is quite disheartening when business leaders once featured on the front of dozens of major magazines are just a few years later being dragged into court and often prison.

Why does this happen?
How can they have fallen?
What corrupted them?

In reality the answer is most likely that they were always corruptible. It's often the case that there were never enough people looking closely enough to catch them out earlier.

We all need to live by a strong moral code. Be very clear about what is right and what is wrong. There should be no shades of grey because often these are places where you falter. What is your moral code? Do you have situations that you have to deal with which could be considered grey? Of course there are differences between moral, ethical and legal codes, but in reality they are closely linked. Once you cross a line, it is a lot easier to keep crossing it and most offenders do.

My philosophy is simple- I will not do anything, ever, that can come back and haunt me. I don't want to ever leave my office with a towel over my head scurrying away from a host of reporters. Apart from the devastating impact it has on your fashion sense it ruins lives, often those of the innocent parties.

What can you do today?

What is your moral code? Do you have areas of grey that need to be clarified once and for all? If you do, clarify them today—even if the ramifications are scary.

Be a fair negotiator

There is a saying that for a negotiation to work, all parties need to win. The level of the win varies, but that is the ideal outcome. Some people adopt an egotistical stance of having to win everything at any cost whenever they enter a negotiation. We all know these kinds of people. They negotiate on the purchase of a bus ticket. They are obsessed with the win, to the point where they spend their life burning other people and, eventually, people don't want to deal with them.

Negotiating is a part of life. In business we need to be good negotiators to make sure we can run our businesses as profitably as possible. But the key word here is fair. I have to negotiate with suppliers, such as graphic designers, media outlets, printers and subcontractors. I want to have a good relationship with these companies and I want them to do the best job possible for my clients. If I screw them down on price to the point where the project is only marginally profitable I will get a marginal job from them and the loser is my client.

I make it clear to my clients from the start: we want to do the best job at the fairest price. If they want a cheaper job done, they have to go somewhere else. This philosophy has enabled me to build for my clients an excellent network of suppliers who do a great job every time. They make good money out of each project, my company makes good money and the client gets the best end result possible.

What can you do today?

What is your philosophy towards negotiating? Are you a fair negotiator or a win-at-any-cost one? The next time you find yourself preparing to enter a negotiation, at any level, take a few minutes to decide how you think all parties can win and work towards this end result. It will make the whole interaction much more enjoyable and the end result will be much better for all parties involved.

Be more than your business

Businesses come and go—what you are doing today is unlikely to be what you will be doing in ten years' time. You are the most significant asset in your life and it is important to realise this.

I encounter a lot of people who become their business—it is everything, from their waking moment in the morning to their last thought at night (and often it fills their dreams).When they no longer have this business their life falls apart.

They don't know what to do, their life feels empty and dissatisfaction and depression can set in.

Look at the lives of a few high-profile entrepreneurs. Rarely do they have only one business interest. They may start new businesses, sell old ones, go broke in some, do a joint venture in others—they are not attached to one business. They are passionate about what they do but they realise they are the resource and the skill centre used to make the other businesses work. They are more than any of the businesses that they own.

Whatever you are doing, there is life after your current business. For this reason you need to be more than your business. You need to have more substance, more interests, more beliefs and more of a long-term view about how you fit into your business life. Don't let your business consume or control you- you are in the driving seat, not the other way around.

What can you do today?

Ponder this thought—what would you do if you got a letter in the mail that said you have to close down your business in 24 hours?
How would you cope, what would you do next?

An interesting situation to spend a few minutes considering.

Have a life outside of your business

We all get absorbed in our businesses and as I have discussed elsewhere in this manual, there is a need for this level of passion and commitment. For many entrepreneurs it comes naturally, but balancing your work life with your personal life can be difficult.

A few years ago I found myself running a growing business. While it wasn't the success I wanted it to be it was well and truly on the way. I had the philosophy that the harder I worked the closer I would be to realising the true potential of the business. So work I did.

Every day I started around 6 a.m. and finished around 9 or 10 at night. I worked seven days a week and I rarely took a day off. I think I became obsessed with what I was doing and this level of obsession is unhealthy. I gained a lot of weight, had a lot of stress, never exercised and I was always tired and run down. A changing point for me came when my sister-in-law died suddenly, at Christmas from a heart attack at the age of 39. Mother of 3 children. I realised I was heading down the same path and I was 39. So I decided to change.

It didn't happen overnight and I have to work on it to this day. But now I feel my life is far more balanced than it has been in a long time. I have lost about 2 stone, I run and walk, eat better, gave up alcohol and I feel great. I start work at about 8 a.m. after having a good breakfast, something I never used to do. I always stop and have a good lunch. I finish in the office by about 5.30 p.m. most days. I rarely work on weekends unless it is absolutely necessary and, then, only if it is work I enjoy doing, like writing books. I pack a lot more into my working day. I am busier now than I have ever been but I have very clear boundaries on when work starts and finishes and where my personal life starts and finishes.

At first the hardest part was to remember what I liked to do; recreation was a strange feeling and one I struggled with. So I made a list of the things I really enjoyed doing— everything from going out to dinner, to seeing a movie, reading and most normal types of recreational pursuit. I put this list in the front of my diary and whenever I felt lost about how to spend my time off I pulled out my list, picked out one of the things I really enjoyed doing and I did it. Over time, my life has got back in balance and I feel great. I run my business better, and there is a good chance I will live longer. I have a lot more friends outside of my business world and they keep my feet firmly planted on the ground. We all need to have a life outside of our businesses as this is what life is all about.

If you have forgotten how, make up your own list, work out how to spend less time at work, and don't hide behind the excuse that you have to be there.

Really, if you have to work seven days a week in your business is it really that profitable?

Is it viable?

Maybe you should be doing something else altogether.

What can you do today?

If your life isn't balanced the way you would like it to be, take steps to change things today. Make a list of the things you used to enjoy doing (and to be even a little more in your face write next to each one the last time you did it). Ring the local gym and get a personal trainer. Do a course that interests you which has nothing to do with business. Remember radical changes like this tend to require a lot of work to make them stick. If you set unreasonable goals it is unlikely to happen so take small steps and work towards your ideal lifestyle.

Be a supporter of other business associates

We all want other people to promote our businesses and to refer customers to us but do we reciprocate and recommend our supporters' businesses to our clients? Doing this often takes a conscious effort but after a while it becomes second nature.

Any kind of recommendation or referral should be a two-way street if possible.

Be clear about which businesses you would like to support and promote them accordingly. It might be quite formal, where you agree to distribute each other's promotional material or do joint advertising or marketing campaigns, or it might be a little more informal—when the opportunity arises you may promote your associates' businesses by word of mouth to your customers.

I have found that the more support I give to other people's businesses the more I get back in return. I don't do it for this reason, that's just an added bonus.

I genuinely want to see these people succeed in what they do and if I can play a small role by referring business to them I will do so gladly.

I also encourage my team to refer businesses wherever possible.

Just like asking your customers to tell their family and friends about what you do, imagine how many referrals will start coming your way if your business associates are doing the same thing. This really is the way of the future for building businesses as it is harder for advertising to make an impact and it is also getting more costly. Direct recommendations are perfect and they are free- the ideal marketing tool.

Think about the people who refer your business. Can you possibly be more active in promoting their businesses? Do it for the right reasons and enjoy the benefits. If you are not 100% sure what they actually do, ask them to come and tell you and your team so you are completely informed.

What can you do today?

Make up a list of businesses you would like to promote. Keep their contact details close to the telephone and wherever possible refer them to your customers as your 'partner' businesses. Try and do this once per day, every day of the coming week.
After a little while it will become a habit.

Mix with people you can learn from

Most entrepreneurs are fairly up-beat kind of people. They are keen to learn and equally keen to pass on their knowledge. Mixing with people who you can learn from is a great way to develop your own business skills and also to pass on your own experiences to help others.

If you mix with smart, successful, enthusiastic people you will become like them if you aren't already. If you are struggling and feeling a little flat, spending time around these people will pick you up and you will do the same for them.

For me I love nothing better than mixing with a group of people who I find stimulating and interesting. Likewise I find nothing worse than mixing with a group of negative, depressed, lacklustre individuals who blame the world for their woes.

Where do you find this group of inspirational souls to mix with?

Talk to people you admire and see what they do. I have found that people like this are already meeting each other either formally or informally all the time. They don't make a

big deal about it; they just do it—a reflection of their lives in general. Invite them for breakfast, lunch or a coffee.
Or make your own group if you can't find one.

With the advent of Internet chat rooms and Skyping you don't even need to be in the same country any more, although it's easier and much nicer to be able to meet face to face. I know a number of people who have formed their own group, consisting of about six people of varying business backgrounds. They meet twelve times every year and spend two sessions brainstorming each of the businesses owned by the people attending. So sometimes you are giving advice, sometimes you are receiving advice, but there is a lot of overlap as often the good advice for another business is just as applicable for your business.

What can you do today?

What type of people do you spend your time with?
Are they positive and good for you or are they a negative influence?
Why not set up your own mentoring group today?
Call five associates that you respect and ask them to be involved.

Make decisions—procrastination is a killer

Personally I find the busier I become, the harder it is to make a decision. I get bombarded with literally hundreds of messages every day, from the phone, email, letters and internally from my team. There is so much to do that finding the time to make a decision on any one thing can be really difficult. But if I don't make decisions, my workload backs up, my clients get frustrated and so do my staff.
A friend of mine who has run some very large corporations pulled me aside a little while ago and gave me some

important advice. She said I had to learn to start making decisions right now; not to keep putting them on the backburner for when I would have more time to think about them. If I did all I would do is end up with an ever expanding list of 'decisions to be made', which I would never get to the end of. I took her advice and she was spot on.

I now make decisions on the spot as often as possible. Some things need a little more time to ponder but in reality the vast majority of my decisions are simple yes or no decisions that someone else needs to action. This has had quite an amazing effect on to my daily workload: it seems I have a lot less to do, I don't go home with a never ending list of things to think about and everyone I deal with is happier because they are getting their decisions quickly. Sure sometimes I make the wrong decisions, but that happened before as well.

We all get it right sometimes and wrong at others but I think the number of wrong decisions I make has declined significantly.

What can you do today?

Do you procrastinate when it comes to making decisions?
End that today.
Get on with it!

Commit to improving your business skills daily

Passionate entrepreneurs seem to have this never ending thirst for ways to do what they do better. They are not afraid to ask questions, to read books, to go to seminars or to learn how to do what they do better. This commitment shines through because they end up putting what they learn into practice.

My guess is that you fit into this category as well; otherwise you wouldn't have invested in this book. But how can you assimilate everything that is on offer considering the mass of information available today and still find the time to run your business and have a life outside of work?
Personally I break it into small bite-sized chunks. My aim is to learn how to do two things better—one for business and one for my personal life—every day of the week.
If I am reading a book on self improvement or business my aim is to find one point I can use today and incorporate that into my business life every day from now on. The same applies to my own personal development—all I want is one point, but I want one every single day of my life.
It is like going to a seminar on business development. It is easy to be bombarded with fifty great things you can do but let's be honest, how many will you get around to actioning?

Probably none...because the task is too daunting.

But if you go into the seminar with a very clear expectation—to take one suggestion that has struck a chord with you and apply it to your business life right now— your chances of achieving this are much higher. I have literally hundreds of business and self-development books. I have read them all and for the most part they are amazing. Filled with thousands of superb ideas and recommendations, but what uses are they if none of them are converted into action by me?

Commit to improving your business and life skills in small manageable chunks. It works for me, and hopefully it will work for you.

What can you do today?

Decide what achievable action you will take to improve your business skills (and hopefully your life skills) on a daily basis. Remember, 'achievable' is the key word here.

Don't be a victim (and keep people who play victim out of your life)

Life throws different blows at all of us and we can choose to focus on these or we can focus on the good things that happen. I'm choosing to focus on the good.

I am not saying for a second there haven't been times when the going got tough, but focusing on the good got me through a lot of situations and a challenging life that many others may not have survived. As a result, I am compassionate and empathetic with anyone going through a rocky patch.

Some people, though, wallow in the role of the victim—everything bad is someone else's fault and they are going to wear the title of 'victim' with pride.

Victims attract other victims and the cycle becomes self-perpetuating. Ironically, I have found that the people who may have the most right to wear a 'victim' badge rarely do. They are too busy getting on with life. The easiest thing for me to do would be to store anger and resentment against a host of people who hurt me, abandoned me or used me.

But without those people I wouldn't have turned out to be who I am today - and I am pretty damn happy with who I am today.

We all face trying times, family problems, relationship problems, money problems and health problems—that is life. But playing victim won't make them go away. Focus on the good things in your life, learn from your experiences and move on. Keep people who play victim out of your life and you will soon find positive and enthusiastic people will replace them—and your life will become a lot better.

What can you do today?

Are you playing victim in your life?
Are there people around you who support the victim mentality?

Well today is the day to throw the victim badge away and get on with your life.

CHAPTER 12
SET THE PACE FOR YOUR COMPETITORS TO FOLLOW

At the start of this manual I explained my thoughts on the future of business and the most obvious and significant piece of advice I can offer on that is that the modern business is extremely competitive and this is a factor that is only going to increase. We all have to deal with competition and I believe this is a good thing not a bad thing.

Competition keeps us trying to be better, it stops us from becoming complacent and it fuels the drive to make our business better than the rest. I also believe customers like the concept of competition. Apart from the obvious reason that it tends to make things more affordable, it also gives people a choice and we all like to have a choice.

There are two ways to look at a highly competitive market: it can be stressful and difficult to make a business successful or it can be an amazing opportunity to drive your business forward. There have been countless examples of businesses entering highly competitive markets and succeeding at quite amazing levels. One of the greatest examples of this in recent times was the introduction of Virgin Airlines, set up and built by Sir Richard Branson.

Virgin quite literally changed the aviation industry in UK by shaking up an industry locked into the 'old way' of doing things and in the process managed to build a strong and loyal clientele in a short amount of time by being innovative. As a by-product, it also made money - something most airlines in the world seem to struggle to do.

The following tips and recommendations are designed to show you how to use your competition to make your business a winning one.

- Believe you are the best and you will become the best
- Enter your business in awards whenever possible
- Get your name in print—there are plenty of opportunities
- Be prepared to get up in front of a crowd—challenge yourself
- Being a green business is good for business
- Be supportive of competitors—even if it is one-sided
- Spend time researching your industry online
- Allow plenty of time to think—and less time to do
- Learn from your mistakes
- Even better, learn from your competitors' mistakes
- Don't become obsessed with your competitors

Believe you are the best and you will become the best

Being the best at what you do has to start with a very firm and genuine belief you can be the best. If you start your business with the aim of being as good as your competitors, that is very noble but far too limiting.

A long time ago I had a business that was really struggling.

A friend sat me down and explained in very simple terms that to be the best you have to do everything better than the competition.

It's a fairly logical thought but it is one that is often not thought through. This may mean shaking old traditions and beliefs and stepping outside of your comfort zone, what is considered the norm in your chosen industry. Believing you are the best is the starting point; from here you need to implement the right actions to make sure you can deliver what you promise and support the concept that you are actually the best at what you do.

With my business at the time, this change in thinking was really the starting point I needed to untangle the mess I had created, and to put a very clear goal and objective into place.

This desire to be the best needs to be imparted to your team, to your suppliers and to your customers. Sure, there will be hurdles to cross, mistakes made and lessons learnt, but you will be heading in the right direction.

What can you do today?

Get a big sheet of paper and write your commitment statement on it: 'I am going to make this the best .... [Whatever your business is]' and sign your name to this commitment. Put your statement on the wall in your office or workshop or place it in a prominent position—where you'll see it constantly.

Enter your business in awards whenever possible

Winning an award is great for business. It gives you recognition, it gives your customers faith in what you do and it motivates the entire team. Everyone loves a winner. There are lots of different awards being run all the time. Some are industry specific, some are geographically specific—it doesn't really matter, an award is an award. Many businesses don't bother entering awards because it can take up quite a bit of time actually filling in the submissions. There are often lots of questions that need to be answered and these can require a reasonable amount of attention.

But entering awards should be considered a marketing activity.

If you are looking for a competitive advantage, being an award winner is certainly one very good boost. If you are fortunate enough to win an award make sure you let everyone know. Put the certificate on your office wall in a prominent place, and make mention of the award on your website and on all of your promotional material. Keeping the certificate in the bottom drawer really is a waste of time and a missed golden opportunity.

I always recommend my clients enter awards wherever possible and those that win really do get quite a lift.

What can you do today?

Is there a submission for an award that you can start working on today?
If you are not sure contact your local government-based Business Advisory
Service—they normally know all about these types of things and they can often even help you to prepare your submission.

Get your name in print- there are plenty of opportunities

There are many benefits from having your name in print. It gives you and your business a lot of credibility, it reinforces to your customers that you know what you are talking about and it generates new business from people who like what you say. The more your name appears in print the more it will appear as your reputation grows.

There are more opportunities to get your name in print today than ever before. There are so many newspapers and magazines and they all need content.

If the editors and journalists can find industry leaders who are prepared to comment on relevant stories or to submit articles there is a good chance those leaders will be published in some format.

The best way to get your name into print is to supply a brief profile outlining who you are and what you do, specifically what areas you feel you're able to offer an informed comment on, to the various publications. It is also a good idea to supply a high resolution electronic version of your photograph (taken professionally) so the publication can publish it with any associated stories.

There are also lots of freelance journalists who are looking for subjects to write articles about. Check the local newspapers and magazines for the names of specific journalists and send them your profile and associated information.

This kind of exposure is relevant at any level—either nationally, internationally or even on the smaller local level. All it takes is a little bit of courage to actually submit your information and accept the fact that you are good at what you do. You are just as qualified as anyone in your industry to make comments.

What can you do today?

Today is a good day to arrange your profile kit and send it out to a number of publications. Start small if that makes you feel more comfortable and build up to the larger, wider-scale opportunities as your confidence grows.

Be prepared to get up in front of a crowd—challenge yourself

For many people the thought of a slow and painful death is preferable to having to stand in front of a crowd and give a talk. As an experienced public speaker I can really relate to this. There are still times when I break into a cold sweat before going on stage. Sometimes it is harder to stand and present in front of a group of 20 people than it is to talk in front of 1000 people. For most of us it is challenging.
I did my first public speaking course when I was at high school and I must say I am very glad I did. I also like to do refreshers every once in a while as I am firmly committed to improving my skills as a public speaker.

The opportunities that public speaking presents are considerable and will give you the opportunity to share your expertise in your chosen field.

There are many situations that call on people to present in a group situation and if you let people know you are prepared to do it, more opportunities will come your way. So take the challenge, face the fear and go for it.

What can you do today?

Anyone can become a better public speaker. Like most skills, though, we need to be taught how. Sign up for a public speaking course that will teach you how to overcome nerves and other insecurities and that will enable you to get up in front of a group of people and share your own knowledge and experiences. Lots of businesses offer these courses. Toast Masters International is one of the most renowned organisations for these types of things but there are plenty to choose from in every country. Even if you are an experienced public speaker your skills can only get better by doing a course like this.

Being a green business is good for business

Running a winning business certainly covers a lot of ground. So far we have discussed corporate imaging, building relationships, customer service, marketing and a host of other topics. But being committed to running an environmentally responsible business is not only good for the environment, it is good for the bank balance—that is a relationship often overlooked.

I have had quite a lot of experience marketing environmentally focused businesses and this is a topic I am passionate about. The point which often amazes me is that green consumers (those who make many of their buying decisions based on environmental responsibility) are growing in numbers rapidly; they are prepared to pay more for green products and services and they are informed and intelligent about those products. Best of all, they are easy to market to because they are looking for environmentally responsible products and services.

If your business is more environmentally aware and responsible than your competitors you will attract customers on this point of difference alone. Of course, if you are an environmentally responsible business you need to tell your customers how you are and what your commitment is.

One excellent example of this is the Body Shop. This impressive organisation has grown to be a leader in beauty products with the main sales point being that the business will not sell any products that don't fit into its stringent corporate philosophy on environmental responsibility and respect for animals. Consumers know that if they purchase a Body Shop product they can rest assured that it has not been tested on animals, a rainforest has not been cut down to produce it or a five-year-old child used in the manufacturing process.

There are lots of ways to be green, far too many to list here. Look at your business from every possible angle and start with small changes, building up to much larger and more significant changes. When your business is environmentally aware you will reap both the moral and financial rewards. One important note here though is, if you are running an environmentally responsible business take the time to explain to your customers what you do to adhere to this code.

This can be in your promotional material, on your website or on a sign in your business. Make sure your team know your philosophy and your commitment.

What can you do today?

Sit down and make a list of five things you could do today to make your business more environmentally responsible.

Then make them happen.

Develop your own environmental philosophy and tell your customers what it is.

Be supportive of competitors- even if it is one-sided

Taking a mature approach to your competitors is a very positive business attribute, even if it isn't reciprocated. In my home town there are quite a few marketing companies, all competing for the same clients, but we have developed a very positive network of referrals and support. My business isn't suited for all clients and if I recognise that a competitor will be better matched to a potential client's needs I have no hesitation in recommending them for the job.

True success comes from rising above petty points of difference and working towards providing the best products and services from the industry as a whole.
The more you work with your competitors the more you will benefit.

It can be very reassuring to sit down with your competitors and talk about business in general. It is nice to know the trials and tribulations you face are also faced by your competitors. But it takes one person to extend the olive branch or to open communication channels. If you already have good relationships with your competitors what can you do to make them even better?

What can you do today?

Make a list of your competitors and write down one sentence that best describes your relationship with each of these businesses. Then write another sentence to say what you could do to have a better relationship.

Spend time researching your industry online

Interestingly this is often an idea overlooked by business owners. It is a very good exercise to spend some time seeing how your industry operates in other countries. Checking out websites from around the world can give you a wealth of information with only a small amount of time spent researching.

The more you explore the more you will find. Use search engines to get the process started but also track down the web addresses of similar companies you may have come across in trade publications.

Not only will you pick up good ideas on building your business but you will more than likely find valuable information about industry trends that could have an impact on your business. If you find out about these trends before your competitors do, your business will be well out in front of the field.
To take this point a little further, it is helpful to print out information you find on the net. Often when you are in a surfing frenzy it is easy to get sidetracked.
Before you know you forget about something you came across earlier.

Collect the information and start a file. Much of the information you come across could probably be distributed among your staff—encourage them to learn from your research.

Spending time to see how other people do the same thing as you is time well spent. Smart entrepreneurs know the value of research and they never begrudge spending time on it. Winning businesses are always one step ahead of their competitors.

What can you do today?

Spend 30 minutes today researching your industry online. Set yourself a challenge to find out something you didn't know before. Start a file and allocate a certain time each week to do nothing but surf the web.

Allow plenty of time to think- and less time to do

Another one of the themes I talk about a lot in this book is the issue of time and the way we all seem to be locked into a constant battle to manage our time.

One of the most serious side effects of this time battle can be that we simply don't find the time to think about our business. We are too busy doing and not busy enough thinking. Taking time out to do nothing but think about your business is therapeutic and beneficial but only if we can make it good quality time.

We all think differently, some people think best in the morning; some at night. Some people need to be in the office to get into the right frame of mind, others need to get away from the office. Personally I think best on a long drive.

Every few weeks I jump into my car, grab my iPod and go for a long drive, maybe for two or three hours up into the Malvern Hills near where I live. There are beautiful, rolling green hills and normally not a lot of traffic. It's relaxing and I find that as soon as I leave the outskirts of town my mind relaxes and I can start to think more clearly. As I drive along I think about the issues at the forefront of my mind, those that are most pressing. As the miles roll by these issues tend to sort themselves out. By the end of my outing I not only feel relaxed, I also feel much clearer and more focused. I have a solution to the issues which I can take back to work and apply on the spot.

This works for me, it might not for you. But what is important here is to find what works for you and use it as often as you can. Sure there is never enough time but you have to make time to think about your business to move it forward, otherwise you may end up stuck in a never changing cycle where business problems are never resolved and opportunities missed because you are too busy just doing the day to day stuff.

What can you do today?

Try and identify when you do your best thinking. Make a list of issues you are struggling to resolve and lock in some time to just think about them.
After a while this will become habit forming and you will look forward to these thinking sessions because you will achieve positive results and your business will move forward.

Learn from your mistakes

Business experience is about making mistakes. I know I have made far more than my fair share, but as the years go by I am getting a little smarter and learning more from my mistakes rather than repeating them.

There wouldn't be a lot of successful entrepreneurs out there who could say they have a mistake-free background. In fact, I would be impressed to meet one.
We all make mistakes and we all will continue to make mistakes- the trick is to learn your lesson and move on.
If you make a business mistake and it costs you money, there is no doubt it will stay in your mind for a long time to come and that is not a bad thing.

There is no point crucifying yourself over a mistake; after all, even the most experienced and high-profile entrepreneurs end up explaining where they went wrong at some stage. Punishing yourself more than necessary is not only non-productive it can also shake your confidence and increase your chances of making more mistakes.
The art of letting go is often easier said than done but it is a skill that will be very beneficial in your business life. Accept the fact that we all make mistakes, learn a lesson, move on and try your hardest not to make the same mistake again.

Where do I get great feedback on what I already offer and what mistakes I'm making?

Online surveys are one of the greatest ways to get anonymous feedback from your customers.
Here are ten reasons 'Why' you'll benefit....

1. Faster

Time is money and you haven't got time to ring, or speak to people face to face to get it done. So sharing the link to the survey when you meet people or via an email campaign is so much easier. The time span needed to complete an online survey project is on average two-thirds shorter than that of a traditional survey method, and a lot less annoying than being stopped in the street on a cold January afternoon. Because the information is being gathered automatically, you don't have to wait for paper questionnaires to come back to you. The response rate is almost instant. Online marketing experts say that more than half the responses are in within the first three days of the research project.

2. Cheaper

Using online questionnaires can halve your research costs. Your business can save money on postage and you don't have to allocate any of your time to enter the information into a database. (Other than the initial questions)The responses are processed automatically and the results are accessible at any time.

3. More accurate

There is a smaller margin of error because clients or customers enter their responses directly into the system. Traditional methods rely on the attentiveness of staff to enter all details correctly, and naturally human error can creep in whenever a person has to perform a repetitive task. (Remember the UK elections…and the amount of recounts and checking and checking of checking?)

4. Quick to analyse

The results of the online survey are ready to be analysed at any time. The data can be presented in graphs or tables, and most online survey tools also offer cross tabulation analysis tools to create contingency tables. You can even hone in on certain questions to see specifics.

5. Easy to use for participants

Ninety percent of people that have access to the Internet prefer to answer surveys online instead of using the telephone. With an online survey, participants can pick a time that suits them best, and the time needed to complete the survey is much shorter. Questions that are not relevant to a particular participant can be skipped automatically.

6. Easy to use for creators

The main benefit of online surveys for creators is that it saves time. The data is instantly available and can easily be transferred into specialised statistical software or spreadsheets when more detailed analysis is needed. There are so many templates that can be used and questions already pre-programmed to copy and paste.

7. Easy to style

An online survey can be styled to match your business or your brand. You can choose the colours and layout of your surveys, and you can add your company logo. You can also add images, audio, or video to the questions in the survey.

8. More honest

Market researchers have found that participants in online surveys usually provide longer and more detailed answers. Because participants feel safe in the anonymous environment of the Internet, they are more likely to open up and give a more truthful response.

9. More selective

With an online survey you can pre-screen participants and allow only those who match your target profile to complete the survey. This way of working allows you to really target specific issues and questions about your business by asking only those who can give you the answers. However, if you want warts and all answers, with 100% integrity, screening your favourite clients, probably isn't the best way of doing things.

10. More flexible

The order of the questions in an online survey can be changed, or questions can be skipped altogether, depending on the answer to a previous question. This way, a survey can be tailored to each participant as he or she proceeds.

Even better, learn from your competitors' mistakes

In the last tip we discussed the importance of learning from your business mistakes and moving on. An even better option is to be a close observer of your competitors and learn from their mistakes.

Albert Einstein's definition of madness is "Doing the same thing over and over again and expect a different result." So based on the man that basically reasoned a majority of our existence, it would be fair to say that a great starting point would be to look at the mistakes of others.

There is just as much to be learnt by entrepreneurs or small business owners who gave up, perhaps just as they were about to become successful.

That must be one of the most annoying things in the world.

Least of all because they either didn't know they were about to be successful or they watched someone else do it instead of them, because they lost their focus of their values, vision and goals.

With that in mind we'll quickly look at some famous names who failed, but we should be fairly glad they didn't give up on their dream, vision or goals.

Before the great Walt Disney built the empire and adventure parks that his estate enjoys today, he was fired by a newspaper editor because "he lacked imagination and had no good ideas."

In 1921, Walt formed his first animation company in Kansas City, where he made a deal with a distribution company in New York, in which he would ship them his cartoons and get paid six months down the road. (Certainly didn't really understand payment terms) He was so broke, he was forced to dissolve his company and at one point could not pay his rent and reportedly ate dog food to keep himself going. (The last bit has been referenced several times, but not entirely sure of the authenticity) Also, When Walt first tried to get MGM studios to distribute Mickey Mouse in 1927, he was told that the idea would never work because a giant mouse on the screen would terrify women.

Whilst I talk of the big screen, world famous and film behemoth, Steven Spielberg was rejected from the University of Southern California School of Theatre, Film and Television a total of three times.

Legendarily when The Beatles were just starting out, their original record label, Decca Recording studios, who had already recorded 15 songs with the group, said "We don't like their sound, and guitar music is on the way out. They have no future in show business."

Steve Jobs was a college dropout, a fired tech executive and an unsuccessful businessman.

At 30-years-old he was left devastated after being unceremoniously removed from the company he founded. Yes that's right, he was fired from Apple.

What can you do today?

Think about your main competitor. What have they done well in the past few months and what have they done poorly?
What lesson can you learn from what they did poorly?
Start reviewing your competitors' mistakes—they are probably doing the same thing of yours.

Don't become obsessed with your competitors

In the last tip I said it was a good idea to look at failure.

We tend to take a keen interest in what our competitors are doing and if you don't you should. Being aware of what is happening within your own market needs to be an accepted part of your business. As you observe your competitors see what they do well and what they do poorly. Clearly both bits of information provide you with an opportunity.

If your competitor makes an obvious mistake—perhaps they have changed their pricing structure and they have out priced themselves, or perhaps their latest advertising is ineffectual or their overall level of customer service has dropped—and you find out about it, their mistake can help your business to grow. This is especially so if you take the time to really think about where they went wrong and what was the main cause of their mistake- did they misread their customers, was there a change of staff or a change of owners or some other key contributing factor.

Mistakes by others. Failures by some.

So here are a few nuggets just to show you what we may never have had if the names in the last section been obsessed with others. They are or were idols in their fields, coming up with some of the most creative things this world has seen. The reason I mention them is that no matter how many times they were told "No", they looked at their goals in a different way, at a different angle to achieve them.

Walt Disney, went ahead and created the infamous 'Chug Boat Willy' cartoon, which introduced the world to Mickey Mouse. So popular did he become that it spawned cartoon after cartoon, feature film after feature film, theme parks and is now worth an estimated $149 Billion, (source Forbes Magazine correct as of May 2014)

Steven Speilberg eventually attended school at another location, only to drop out to become a director before finishing.

Thirty-five years after starting his degree, Spielberg returned to school in 2002 and actually completed his BA. "I wanted to accomplish this for many years as a thank-you to my parents for giving me the opportunity for an education and a career, and as a personal note for my own family- and young people everywhere- about the importance of achieving their college education goals." On a personal note can we also thank-you Steven for giving us Indiana Jones, Back to the Future and Jurassic Park.

The Beatles, went onto record 17 UK number ones and sold a staggering 600 million albums worldwide. So I guess the accountants at Decca will always be rueing the band that got away.

And in a 2005 speech at Stanford University, Jobs explained, "I didn't see it then, but it turned out that getting fired from Apple was the best thing that could have ever happened to me. The heaviness of being successful was replaced by the lightness of being a beginner again, less sure about everything. It freed me to enter one of the most creative periods of my life."

After his return to Apple, Jobs help create several iconic products, including the iPod, iPhone and iPad, which have in all seriousness, has completely changed the consumer electronics arena forever. Oh and Jobs became one of the richest men in the world.

The reason I point these very famous figures out, is because we only really know them for the successes they became and not the failures that some thought they were. The simple fact that they were tenacious enough to carry on when people told them "No" and the fact they learnt from mistakes they had made, in my eyes made them more likely to succeed than fail. Many of us throw our 'toys out of the cot' when we are told "No" or realise we have "failed" at something, and a majority of people give up and try something else.

Imagine if Steve Jobs for example had gone onto to become a world fly fisher. (You never know...but bear with me here). Apple was struggling big time when they asked him back. Some reports suggest any longer it would have gone out of business and companies like Microsoft would have been king. There would have been NO iPod. NO iPad. No iPhone. Can we honestly say that the world would have been the same without them? They were so far ahead of anything anyone else was doing, it was revolutionary. It changed the way we listened to music through iTunes. It changed the way we operated office programmes, watched TV, video and read books. It changed the way we communicated with each other through mobile, texting, messaging and Face Time. They are responsible for so many things we now take for granted.

CHAPTER 13
16 BASIC LAWS THAT EVERY BUSINESS SHOULD FOLLOW

Every business is governed by 'laws' and not necessarily the laws of Government. These are more laws that every successful business on the planet follow in some shape or form.

They seem at first glance quite easy, but it's amazing how many businesses try to be clever and make running a business harder than it really needs to be. Look at them in their simplest form and see which ones you are missing or trying to make too complicated. If you're making them too complicated, you're also probably spending too much money or wasting too much time in that area. Remember the song sung by Bobby Fuller, "I fought the law and the law won." Never a truer word spoken!

1 The law of perception.

Business and marketing in general are a battle of perceptions and not simply a battle of products. The best product doesn't always win. But the perception of a good business and product will always win.

2 The law of questions.

Questions lead to answers; answers lead to relationships; relationships lead to profit.

When was the last time you asked questions of your customers, your colleagues or your peers? You haven't got all the answers, but by asking questions, opportunities and new ideas will appear. Just listen to the answers!

3 The law of precision.

The ability to accurately define your precise market segments dramatically affects your profitability. So segment clearly and carefully. Stop trying to sell to everyone because it spreads you too thinly.

4 The law of different missions for different positions.

Your strategies depend on your position. You can't have the same approach to someone that is a first time buyer when talking to a person that buys from you regularly.

5 The law of time.

Marketing and business exist in the long term. It's all about relationships. Building them; maintaining them; rebuilding them; maintaining them some more...You get the idea. Not everyone is ready to buy now, but the key over time is to be number one in their mind when it comes to that decision.

6 The integration law.

Marketing is worth nothing if it is not companywide. Everyone has to be singing from the same hymn sheet when it comes to company values and its marketing. The marketing should seamlessly represent what the business is about and what it offers.

7 The law of the driving seat.

The management team is the centre for improvement, drive it from the top.

Question. Why should the team improve if the people running the business don't?

It's the quickest way to become detached from your workforce, your customers and reality. Ever heard of the saying, "Don't ask people to do something if you are not willing to do it yourself"? It's true. Many systems that are implemented by management, when they get to the shop floor don't work. Why? Because management have been sold an idea or ideal that is far removed from the reality of what happens daily. Watch an edition of 'Undercover Bosses' and see for yourself the amount of back tracking management really have to do.

8 The law of measurement.

Don't just measure improvement. You can measure anything. Measure the things you want to improve as well as measure what works really well and see if you can do more of it.

9 The first law.

If you are not number one in your existing category then create your own category, or be the first in their minds. (Look at law 3)

10 The law of tricky extensions.

The irresistible urge to extend product lines or move into new markets may be self-defeating in the long run - brand equity, when stretched usually gets spread more thinly. In other words don't expand and grow into different areas unless you've done the proper groundwork and your existing business is protected.

11 Pareto's Law.

The 80:20 rule is everywhere. But in case you don't already know it, it's that 80% of you sales and profit comes from 20% of your customers and clients. So to be effective, cut back on the ineffective and focus on the effective efforts.

12 The law of success and failure.

Success and failure go hand-in-hand - it's OK to make mistakes but learn from them; and remember nothing succeeds like success.

13 The law of reversibility.

Start with the end in mind, and accept responsibility for the results, or don't bother starting.

14 The 'P-FAB-P' law.

Customers buy benefits and proofs - show them the advantages and features but make sure the benefits and proofs address their problem.

15 The law of tolerance.

The customer is always right. They may also be misguided, ill-informed, delusional, rude, and ignorant plus a bad attitude. But they are always right. They pay money for your products and services and in turn pay for your lifestyle. Tolerance is something that can be learned and practiced.

16 The law of KISS.

Keep It Simple Stupid. Make your product or service easy to use and easy to buy and customers will keep coming back.

CHAPTER 14

110 QUESTIONS TO ASK YOU AND YOUR BUSINESS

ANSWERS CONSTANTLY CHANGE

As you've probably seen throughout the book, I do like to ask questions.

It's a coach's job to ask those questions and then get you to hear the answers to them, and then maybe get you to 'reframe' those answers in the context of whatever we're talking about. It's key you 'hear' the answers to questions. By hearing I mean, actually taking notice, responsibility and ownership of the answers.

In general we are all happy to listen to positive answers to questions. Such as, "Are you brilliant at what you do?", "Yes I am". But none of us are very good at hearing this answer to the same question; "You are good but you could do this, this and this to be brilliant." Many of us will hang on to the "You are good..." and then mutter under our breath about the fact they didn't think we were brilliant. Not many people would listen to the "..But you could do this, this and this..." bit of the conversation. And that's a shame. Because winning businesses listen to those nuggets of information, act upon it and grow themselves and their businesses because of it.

So when I wrote this bit there were 75 questions I originally asked of my business and of myself. As you can see these increased by nearly 50% when I found that I wanted to drill down even more and be as honest with myself as I could be.

Now that you've got through this book and have already started answering questions as honestly as you can, these 110 questions will not only get you to think on things you already maybe thinking about, but also get you to drill down even further and think about you as the business leader. Answer honestly and openly.

1. What business are you in?

2. Where do you make your money?

3. Is my product / service a real business?

4. How good are you at your competitive positions?

5. Is this a good industry to be in?

6. What do your clients think?

7. How do you raise profits quickly?

8. How do you build long term value?

9. Who / What business inspires your business?

10. What do you do differently from other businesses?

11. What investments underpin your differences?

12. What are your key sources of competitive advantage?

13. What do you need to do to make a difference?

14. What must you keep?

15. What must you lose?

16. How could you simplify your business so that you can raise its value by 50%?

17. How could you simplify your business so that you could lower your costs by 10%?

18. Is your strategy rather complex? Aren't all successful businesses strategies very simple?

19. What is the key idea to your business concept?

20. Who is your target client?

21. What do you know about them?

22. Can you describe your perfect client in detail?

23. Where do they hang out?

24. What do they read?

25. How do they interact socially?

26. What problem are you solving for your customers?

27. How much power do your clients and customers have over your business?

28. Why do people buy your product at all?

29. Why do people buy your product from you?

30. Why does your typical client buy from you?

31. Which clients are cool?

32. Which clients drive you mad?

33. Should you be working with them?

34. What benefits are you offering that your competition doesn't?

35. If you could use just two sentences to describe what your business stands for, what would they be?

36. What is your company known for?

37. What's your value proposition to clients that they can't get elsewhere?

38. Who are your most profitable clients?

39. At what rate do they leave you?

40. Why do they leave you?

41. Who is your most serious competitor?

42. What are their plans?

43. Do you really know what clients think of you?

44. Is the customer always right?

45. What are your competitor's costs and profits?

46. Who are currently your new/minor threats?

47. Are you supplying the right things?

48. And the most effective way?

49. At the lowest possible economic cost?

50. How much does your business use in technology in comparison with your competitors?

51. Are your assumptions in the last set of questions, still valid? When did you last check?

52. How much power do your suppliers have over your business?

53. Are you as good, or better than your best competitor?

54. Are you serving the widest possible market?

55. Are you in some way unique? Is there a reason why people should buy from you rather than someone else?

56. Would your God have a laugh at your marketing plan?

57. What keeps you awake at night about your business?

58. What are your objectives for your business?

59. What are you trying to achieve in the next 12 months?

60. What are you trying to achieve in the next 3 years?

61. What is the vision for your business in 5 years?

62. What barriers are in your way to achieve your goals in the next 12 months?

63. What will enable you to overcome the barriers, and/or achieve your goals?

64. If you had a magic wand, what changes would you make to your business?

65. What is stopping you from making those magic wand changes now?

66. Are all incentives aligned with your business goals?

67. What are the three most critical things to the success of the business?

68. Which 20% of clients account for the 80% of profit?

69. Who are your top five clients and how much contribution did they generate last month?

70. Which clients are unprofitable?

71. Which clients would you sack?

72. Which underperforming products / services should you drop now? Why?

73. Which products / services should you concentrate on selling more of?

74. What is success for you?

75. What is success for your business?

76. What does your business stand for?

77. Is the work you do, dull or exciting?

78. So what is it that you do that is so exciting?

79. Does it matter?

80. How do you raise the impact?

81. What will be your legacy?

82. Are you thinking big enough?

83. Are you pushing, leading or goading your clients?

84. If your business was an animal, what would it be and why?

85. What animal would you like it to be and why?

86. What do you need to do to get your business from being the animal it is, to become the animal that you want it to be?

87. If your business were an island, what sort of island would it be?

88. Running your business is like riding a bicycle because…

89. If you could work half time, what would you do to double your profit?

90. What would Sir Richard Branson do if he took over your business?

91. What would your closest rival do if they took over your business?

92. How can you get luckier?

93. What excuses do you use?

94. Do you have the right people around you?

95. Would your business run day-to-day without you?

96. What contingency plans have you got in place should you become ill and need to take a year off?

97. Do you avoid tough decisions?

98. Do you feel burned out?

99. How committed are you to the business?

100. How committed are you to your vision and personal goals?

101. When was the last time you set yourself a personal goal, that wasn't boring?

102. When was the last time you set yourself a business goal, that wasn't boring?

103. When was the last time you did some business training? Boosted your own capabilities?

104. Are you always right?

105. When was the last time you got someone to look at your business from a different perspective?

106. If Lord Alan Sugar came into your business today, what would he tell you was wrong with your business?

107. How could you do less of it?

108. If Lord Alan Sugar came into your business today, what would he tell you was right with your business?

109. How could you do more of it?

110. How could you improve it?

THE LAST WORD
SWING FOR THE FENCE OR SMASH IT OUT OF THE GROUND

From a young age, I loved the idea of starting a business. I guess it helps that during the recession of the 1980's I watched my father struggle and my mother hold down three jobs to keep a roof over our head and food on the table. I thank my mum for everything she did. She showed that when your back is up against the wall, you will fight, tooth and nail to 'get by'. You can fight to get to the light at the end of the tunnel. I know my mum gave up a lot of her dreams and needs, just so we could get by.

I will thank my dad. But I'm going to thank him for teaching me two very early lessons in entrepreneurship. Pick your moment. Pick your product. And if you do believe in what you're doing; go after it; look at it from different positions; from different angles. Just don't give up and resent the failure. He did. It was painful. He was mentally hurt by those years. His reaction hurt our family. Always worked hard, but I'm fairly certain he only ever 'just got by'. It's not a place I want to go. It's a place that people with passion for their projects and their business should never go.

I was going there until the age of 38 and then started following my dreams and doing things I knew I could do. Since then, I've launched several ideas. Some succeeded, and some failed. While I made and lost money, each success or failure always led me to learn something new.

So, looking back over my career, in management and as a business owner, I looked at lessons I wish I'd known or have learnt the hard way when I started out.

There are also circumstances that dictate the way you come at businesses and what perspective you look at them. My example of doing what I'm doing now shows that retrospective thinking or analysis can be the spur of success.

Here's the deal: it takes as much effort to create a small company as it does to create a large one, so you might as well swing for the fences and smash it out of the ground.

What do the successful businesses look like?

Well, the first question you have to ask is this: are you are a slugger or a base hitter?

If I were to use cricketing terms, it would be are you six hitter like Ian Botham or a 'nurdler' like the infamous Geoff Boycott?

In other words, what is your tolerance for risk *versus* reward?

What businesses would you like to emulate and be more successful than?

Remember employees and to a point franchisees are 'base hitters and nurdlers'. They don't really want to take the risks. They want to be safe from the genuine risks, but survive off the rewards that your risk entails.

Entrepreneurs, on the other hand, can be sluggers and six hitters. While CEOs of national, multi-national or global companies can make big money, most of the millionaires in the world tend to be entrepreneurs. As the world economies go into recession, then develop, ebb and flow, history always points to the brave entrepreneurs that succeed.

So the question is... where do you want to be?

Well I'm going to leave you with this one, which goes to show you...the entrepreneur, the business owner, the manager, the CEO; whoever you are...is only one decision away from greatness.
Give up or go for it.

It's yours if you want it....

I want to leave you with a story that shows if you put some and hopefully all, of this book into practice; business is just as much a mental game as it is a facts, figures, beliefs and processes one. This story comes courtesy of an excellent morning spent in the company of Andy Cope, he of the 'Art of Brilliant' fame and some amazing primary school teachers.

If you haven't already done so, go out and buy a copy of the 'Art of Brilliant' or 'Be Brilliant Everyday' and apply some of the strategies to your everyday life, but go one step further and apply some of the strategies to your business.

For those that don't know of the 'Art of Brilliant', Andy is one part of a writing team, that along with Andy Whitaker, have written books, encouraging the readers to be brilliant in everyday life. Andy Cope is the part of the partnership that has effectively a degree in happiness or the psychology of happy. He's studied it over the last 10 years and has invested thousands of hours studying the '2%ers'. (Andy Whittaker, by his own admission, is just a bloke from Mansfield, but writes the funny bits.)

The'2%ers' are the 2% that are happy and content with life.

In direct correlation of the happy 2% in the world, I would suggest is the top 2% in business. Remember there is an actual fact, that 90% of the world wealth is controlled by 2% of the population. (You also have to believe that money does make you happy...if it doesn't, it certainly helps.) I was really interested in hearing what the main key point of 10 years worth of research was and it was put simply as this: the number one thing that positive people do to make themselves happy, upbeat and full of life is......drum roll please..... They CHOOSE to be happy!

The Art of Brilliant even states: "All the happy, upbeat, extraordinary people that were surveyed and studied made a conscious decision to lead a positive life. This conscious choice to be positive and upbeat doesn't make the sun shine or the traffic disappear, but it does put them in a better frame of mind to deal with the stuff that life inevitably throws in their direction. By actively choosing to be positive, people are better able to attack issues with real purpose, vigour, enthusiasm and are more likely to come up with solutions."

And I can't disagree. So let's translate this to the world of business. Business lives intersect with our personal lives and some of the most successful people on the planet have the same issues as small business people; the difference is it's just a scalable problem.

Could it be that positive mental attitude is the difference between businesses that are winners or ones that are just mediocre and surviving?

Is it as simple as choosing to be positive and successful? Maybe not, but it's a start.

Being positive in every aspect of your business can put you onto a road destined for better than most and heading for the '2%ers'.

A phrase that did keep coming up is the phrase, 'Being the best you that you can be.' Let's place that idea into your business.

So let's do a quick task.

- What 3 things do you think your business is brilliant at, when it's at its best?

- What 3 things do you think your business is not great at when it's being mediocre and the same as everyone else?

Now you've got two lists. Which one do you prefer?
I think I know the answer to that.

What can you do today?

Which list are you going to consciously be?
Then tomorrow, which list are you going to consciously be?
And the day after?

What I'm trying to get at is if you want a world class and successful business, you and your team need to consciously make a decision, and own that decision, to be the best business that you can be daily.

One of the questions that were asked during the morning was 'What Superhero are you when you're at your best?" The primary school teachers were saying things like Spider-Man, Wonder Woman and stuff like that. I came up with Danger Mouse, simply because throughout my career I'd always be followed by a 'Penfold' character that said, "Crumbs chief, what do we do now?"

Andy went on to suggest Bob the Builder was in fact a superhero for modern times.

Got to be honest; I wasn't sure about this one, but his explanation was absolutely on the money.
He's watched the entire box set and noticed two things. (He has children.) Now if you're a builder and you did this, you'd be amazing and slot straight into the 2% in my opinion.

Firstly from a customer point of view, he NEVER, EVER goes to a job, purses his lips and complains about dodgy work, the state of things or asks people to stick the kettle on whilst he adds things to the bill, because you didn't tell him the technical stuff he really needed to know over the phone. Let's be fair, who would? You're not the builder; he is.

Secondly, how many stories have you heard from people that builders have over run or are taking their time in their opinion? Or they're asking for money because they underestimated what was needed? Or they've done a runner because it was too difficult? Well if you watch the programme, there is always that moment in the episode where something has gone wrong. The moment of impending 'child level' doom, where the project is about to fall apart. But guess what? All Bob says is, "Can we fix it?" And his team shout back "Yes we can!"

That there ladies and gentlemen is a winning team...a team that is choosing to be positive in the face of something happening to them and their project. And the 'customer' ends up happy and they all toddle off and have tea and cakes somewhere.

The more you do it, the more positive things will happen for you, for your customers and for your business. Just by being 'wowed' by you, means your customers / clients are going to love you more. If they love you more, the more they'll tell their friends. The more business will come your way.

That's what being brilliant taught me. Being the best version of my business means the best version of my business that my clients will see and feel.
I'm aiming to be a '2%er'- the happier, positive, can do kind of business. The best business I can be.

What about you?

Stuff that is always at the end

Books Discussed in this book are:
Guerrilla Marketing, Jay Conrad
How to Win Friends and Influence People, Dale Carnegie
First Stops to Wealth, Dani Johnson
Fish, Stephen Lundin
Start With Why, Simon Sirnek
The Art of Being Brilliant and Be Brilliant Everyday, Andy
Cope and Andy Whittaker.
(Available in good bookshops and not so good bookshops
probably)

Clothing colour piece provided by Tanisha Degutis:
She has a bachelor degree in costume design, worked
alongside famous European designers, couture pieces sold
in European boutiques as well as writing pieces featured in
magazines and news papers throughout Europe.
Follow her on Twitter @TanishaDegutis

Visit our website for blogs, ideas, tips and strategies;
contact us and get free stuff:

www.marcford.uk